HOCKEY SUPERSTITIONS

Andrew Podnieks is the author of more than fifty-five books on hockey. The following is a select list:

Canadian Gold: 2010 Olympic Winter Games Ice Hockey Champions

Honoured Canadiens

Players: The Ultimate A-Z Guide of Everyone Who Has Ever Played in the NHL

The Complete Hockey Dictionary

World of Hockey: Celebrating a Century of the IIHF

A Day in the Life of the Maple Leafs

Canada's Olympic Hockey History, 1920-2010

A Canadian Saturday Night

Portraits of the Game: Classic Photographs from the Turofsky Collection at the Hockey Hall of Fame

The NHL All-Star Game: Fifty Years of The Great Tradition

ANDREW PODNIEKS

HOCKEY SUPERSTITIONS

FROM PLAYOFF BEARDS TO CROSSED STICKS AND LUCKY SOCKS

McClelland & Stewart

Library and Archives Canada Cataloguing in Publication

Podnieks, Andrew
Hockey superstitions : from playoff beards to crossed
sticks and lucky socks / Andrew Podnieks.

ISBN 978-0-7710-7108-9

1. Hockey—History—Miscellanea. 2. Superstition. I. Title.

GV846.5.P624 2010   796.962   C2010-901567-3

We acknowledge the financial support of the Government of Canada
through the Book Publishing Industry Development Program and that
of the Government of Ontario through the Ontario Media Development
Corporation's Ontario Book Initiative. We further acknowledge the support
of the Canada Council for the Arts and the Ontario Arts Council for our
publishing program.

Published simultaneously in the United States of America by McClelland &
Stewart Ltd., P.O. Box 1030, Plattsburgh, New York 12901

Library of Congress Control Number: 2010927463

Typeset in Palatino by M&S, Toronto
Printed and bound in Canada

ANCIENT FOREST
FRIENDLY

This book was produced using ancient-forest friendly papers.

McClelland & Stewart Ltd.
75 Sherbourne Street
Toronto, Ontario
M5A 2P9
www.mcclelland.com

1 2 3 4 5   14 13 12 11 10

CONTENTS

Introduction 1

GROUP SUPERSTITIONS *Universal Tribalism*

The Playoff Beard 7
The Playoff Beard Gains Momentum 9
The Playoff Beard Reaches the Owner's Box.. 10
To Lift or Only to Smile? 11
Don't Touch Stanley Unless You've Earned the Right 13
Change of Numbers, Change of Luck... 15
Sticks: The Wand Is Pure Magic 17
Pyramid Power.. 19
Kate Smith... 21
Don't Follow Death... 24
Detroit's Octopus 26
Crappiest Superstition Ever 28
Stan the Man 30
The Net Is Sacred.. 31
The March to War... 34
Last Taps.. 35
A Magical Few Weeks.. 37
The Mascot 38
Order of Dress... 40
A Good Cob 41
The Lucky Loonie... 43
Eat Right 45
A Coach's Tie.. 46
That's Not a Rug 50
The Lucky Butt of L.A. 52
Referees Are People, Too 53
Superstitions on Air 54
Fandemonium.. 55

PLANE SUPERSTITIONS *To Each His (Crazy) Own*

PLAYER SUPERSTITIONS *To Each His (Crazy) Own*

KARL ALZNER: Crazy Eights... 61
SERGE AUBRY: Sartorial Exorcism....................................... 62
ED BELFOUR: *Noli Me Equipment Tangere*........................ 63
BILL BEVERIDGE: Hey, Buddy... 64
PETER BONDRA: Counting One to Five.............................. 65
Quick Shot: **DANIEL BOUCHARD**... 67
BRUCE BOUDREAU: Groundhog Day................................... 67
RAY BOURQUE: Lace 'Em Up, Over and Over.................... 69
JOHNNY BOWER: Ancient Beliefs....................................... 70
DARREN BOYKO: Time to Worry.. 71
DANIEL BRIÈRE: Do Unto Other Sticks As You Would Have Them Do Unto You....... 72
MARTIN BRODEUR: Family and Hockey Can Coexist............ 73
PETER BUDAJ: D'oh... 74
GERRY CHEEVERS: Better the Mask than the Face............ 75
Quick Shot: **CHRIS CHELIOS**... 77
JACQUES CLOUTIER: Red Is the Colour of Victory............. 78
SIDNEY CROSBY: Sorry, Mom, Can't Talk......................... 78
WILF CUDE: Rabbit's Foot—or Not................................... 80
Quick Shot: **JOE DALEY**.. 81
GERRY DESJARDINS: Personal GPS at Work...................... 81
SHANE DOAN: Good Player, Good Book............................ 82
KEN DRYDEN: Smart, but Superstitious All the Same........ 84
PHIL ESPOSITO: Lord, There Goes a Scorer..................... 86
TONY ESPOSITO: Just Let Them Be.................................. 88
Quick Shot: **BOB ESSENSA**... 90
RAY FERRARO: Chicken Parm for All Times....................... 90
Quick Shot: **BOB GAINEY**... 91
Quick Shot: **BERT GARDINER**... 92
BRUCE GARDINER: Potty Trained....................................... 92
BOYD GORDON (and **MATT BRADLEY**): A Most Delicate Touch....... 94
SCOTT GORDON: Get a Grip.. 95
"RED" GOUPILLE: The Real Thing...................................... 96
Quick Shot: **RON GRAHAME**... 97
"CAMMI" GRANATO: What a Doll.. 98

"WIN" GREEN: Trained to Win (or Tie) 99

WAYNE GRETZKY: Not Too Good for the Rest of Us 100

GLENN HALL: The Fine Art of Upchucking 102

DOUG HARVEY: Always a Close Shave 103

Quick Shot: **JOHAN HEDBERG** 105

BRYAN HELMER: Tells a Good Story 105

PAUL HENDERSON: Even Heroes Believe 106

RON HEXTALL: Smack, Boom, Bang! 107

DALE HUNTER: Lucky Horse Blanket 109

"PUNCH" IMLACH: The Fearful Dictator 110

GARY INNESS: Just Relax 112

Quick Shot: **JAROMIR JAGR** 113

PETR KLIMA: One and Done 113

GUY LAPOINTE: Messing with a Superstition 115

GEORGE LARAQUE: Here a Bump, There a Bump 116

STÉPHAN LEBEAU: Game Day by the Clock 117

PELLE LINDBERGH: Pripps, Please 118

DOUG MACLEAN: Four-Leaf Clover 119

KEITH MAGNUSON: Green Means Go, and Green Means Win 120

EVGENI MALKIN: Playing Footsie 121

CESARE MANIAGO and the Lucky Sock 122

Quick Shot: **"MUSH" MARCH** 124

JOHN MCINTYRE: Alpha and Omega 124

KYLE MCLAREN: Clueless in San Jose 125

SAMMY MCMANUS: No Number 13, No Matter What 126

Quick Shot: **GILLES MELOCHE** 127

MARK MESSIER: Don't Worry 128

STAN MIKITA: Butt, Of Course 129

ALFIE MOORE: Hat/No Hat 131

JUSTIN MORNEAU: Roy's Biggest Fan 134

LOU NANNE: Same As It Ever Was 135

RICK NASH: Too Many, Too Private 136

BERNIE NICHOLLS: "Pumper-Nicholl" and Twig 136

Quick Shot: **JOE NIEUWENDYK** 138

BOBBY ORR: Even the Greatest Make Believe 138

MIKE PALMATEER: The Popcorn Kid 141

BERNIE PARENT: Phantom of the Crease 142

Quick Shot: **COREY PERRY** 144

Quick Shot: **JACQUES PLANTE**......................................144
Quick Shot: **FÉLIX POTVIN**......................................145
Quick Shot: **STÉPHANE QUINTAL**...............................145
CRAIG RAMSAY: Two to Be Good 146
Quick Shot: **BILL RANFORD** 147
"CHICO" RESCH: Baby, Don't You Drive That Car 147
LUC ROBITAILLE: Tales of the Tape 148
PATRICK ROY: Herky-Jerky Quirky 151
GEOFF SANDERSON: The Long and Short of It................153
Quick Shot: **LAURIE SCOTT**.....................................154
EDDIE SHORE: Feared and Afraid..............................155
Quick Shot: **GARY SIMMONS**....................................156
Quick Shot: **CHRIS SIMON**......................................156
Quick Shot: **ALEX SINGBUSH** 156
Quick Shot: **TYLER SLOAN**......................................157
GARY SMITH: Dressing, Dressing, Dressing Room...........157
CONN SMYTHE: A Real Screamer..............................158
Quick Shot: **DOUG SOETAERT**..................................159
MATS SUNDIN: No Triskaidekaphobia Here 160
MAXIME TALBOT: Whole Lotta Believin' 162
JOCELYN THIBAULT: Calming Down 163
WAYNE THOMAS: Now That's Quick............................165
Quick Shot: **"TINY" THOMPSON**................................166
Quick Shot: **MARK TINORDI** 166
JOHN TONELLI: A Little Spit 167
Quick Shot: **LOUIS TRUDEL**.....................................168
DARCY TUCKER: Same Old, Same Old 168
RON TUGNUTT: Move It or Lose It 169
MARTY TURCO: What Was He Thinking? 171
Quick Shot: **ROGIE VACHON**....................................172
STEVE VALIQUETTE: Insane in the Membrane..............172
PHIL WATSON: Believe It or Not 174
Quick Shot: **BERNIE WOLFE**....................................175

Acknowledgements *177*
Photo Credits *179*

INTRODUCTION

TO SOME LESSER OR GREATER DEGREE, we are all creatures of habit and we all have rituals of one sort or another. The lowest form might be called habit, while a grade higher might be called tradition. And then there is superstition, the highest and most serious kind of ritual.

Habits are simple to understand and define. One person has a habit of twirling his key chain as he walks along the street; another is in the habit of whistling while she drives to work. But superstition might be defined as necessary habit. Someone who believes he will be hit by a car if he doesn't twirl his key chain is out-and-out superstitious. The woman who whistles on her drive to work because she believes she won't get pulled over for speeding if she does so is equally superstitious.

Over time, some habits turn into superstitions, consciously or not. Every finance minister has bought a new pair of shoes before delivering a budget because he was following a tradition of superstition. Those who hold their breath while driving by a cemetery or who avoid walking under a ladder are superstitious for reasons that, honestly, make little sense.

Some people are superstitious because they are not superstitious. Hugh Campbell, one of the greatest coaches in Canadian Football League history, once told it to me like this when I asked him if he were superstitious. "No, not at all," he said, "but so many people are that if they send me a good-luck charm and tell me to put it on my desk, I do because there's no point in messing with someone's superstition." Ergo, he has his own form of non-superstition superstition!

Hockey players are superstitious because they are first creatures of habit. But over time, if those habits take them from house league to the National Hockey League, these simple habits take on greater meaning. "I've always put my equipment on the same way," a player might say, "and since it got me to the NHL, there's no point in changing how I dress."

Therein lies the subtext, the unspoken meaning. Superstitions are merely habits that players use to create positive self-esteem, to make them feel like if they do this and this, they will succeed. If players can execute a series of actions that will help them relax and make them feel like they will play better, then they *will* play better because they have given themselves a psychological boost.

Some superstitions stay with players their whole career; others change as often as need be to explain away a loss or understand a great game. Of course, fans also have superstitions—a favourite chair to watch the game in, a select group of friends to watch it with, a particular meal to eat when a win is required.

Deep inside, though, every player—every person —knows superstitions are thin as onion skin. They don't really determine a good game or bad, success or failure. But anything players can find and use to help them feel better, and, therefore, play better, is required conditioning at the highest level. Superstitions are silly, funny, and ridiculous, but if a player says they work, then they do!

Andrew Podnieks

GROUP SUPERSTITIONS
Universal Tribalism

The usually clean shaven Denis Potvin, like most of his teammates, refused to shave during the playoffs with the New York Islanders in the early 1980s.

THE PLAYOFF BEARD

The playoff beard is a sure and ubiquitous sign that Stanley Cup hockey has arrived. For a dozen games in the pre-season of September through the eighty-two gruelling games that comprise the regular season, the NHL's nearly one thousand players are clean-shaven, with a few sporting a beard year-round and only a handful even crafting a moustache. But when the calendar turns to the first day of the playoffs, all players on all sixteen playoff teams put away their razors, vowing not to shave again until they have won the Stanley Cup (or, more likely, have been eliminated).

The playoff beard has come to mean several things. First, it is about the team, a way of bonding and showing each teammate that the players are "all for one and one for all" as they begin the quest for hockey's Holy Grail. Furthermore, it is about perseverance, about each player making a collective vow not to shave, not to care about personal appearance or tonsorial etiquette because looks don't matter, family doesn't matter, nothing matters except chasing the dream for the next two months of hockey.

Because the beard is not a feature players enjoy the rest of the year, it is also a symbol for the suffering they are willing to endure to win. Wearing a beard, especially in the spring and summer months when the playoffs are scheduled, is as unpleasant in its own way as blocking a shot, losing a tooth, or sticking up for a teammate during a game.

The beard is an outward commitment by the players to their fans that they are willing to do whatever it takes to win in the playoffs, willing to vouchsafe all personal cleanliness and focus only on bringing home the Cup. It acts as a constant reminder to each player of this promise, this dedication.

Dave Lewis, a member of the New York Islanders from 1973 to 1980, believes that his team started the NHL tradition of the playoff beard in the mid-1970s. However, photographs of the team from those playoffs don't consistenly corroborate his claim. It seems to have begun with the Islanders, to be sure, but not until 1980, when the team won the first of four straight Cups (1980–83). Lewis, unfortunately, was traded to Los Angeles late in the 1979–80 season and never won a championship with the team.

The 1979–80 team that won the Cup for the first time featured two Swedes—Stefan Persson and Anders Kallur—the first Europeans to win the Stanley Cup (Bob Nystrom, also on the team, was born in Sweden but grew up in Canada).

Another irrefutable fact is that Swedish tennis king Björn Borg began a Wimbledon tradition of growing a beard back in 1976. Each Wimbledon he started clean-shaven, vowing not to touch a razor again until the end of the tournament. He won five championships in a row, and each trophy presentation featured a bearded Borg accepting the prize (Andy Roddick tried to mimic this habit in 2008, but he failed to win the lawn championship). It is well within reason to think the Swedish players copied their national legend and brought the beard tradition to the NHL.

THE PLAYOFF BEARD GAINS MOMENTUM

The successful run of four Stanley Cup wins in a row with bearded superstitions established the New York Islanders in the game's history, but that doesn't mean the legend spread from that day to this. Indeed, the team's success more or less ended the playoff beard for some time. The Edmonton Oilers took over from the Isles as the dominant team for the rest of the 1980s, and those players refused to copy a tradition possibly started by their rivals (many of their great players were probably also too young to grow truly Grizzly Adams–ish beards anyway). So, the Oilers won their Cups with clean-shaven faces and lightning speed and skill.

Ironically, while the New York Rangers would never dare do anything similar to the Islanders—or vice versa—it seems that the beard returned with the New Jersey Devils in 1988, the first year that previously sad-sack team made the post-season. Their beards didn't grow long before they were eliminated, but in 1995, the team continued with the tradition, won the Cup, and never looked back.

Momentum picked up as the century came to a close, and now, far from worrying about copying an enemy's habit, the superstition is that you can't win the Cup without adopting the team beard philosophy. Ergo, the evolution to today when players on all sixteen teams grow their beards and every spring one team does, indeed, win the Stanley Cup with full beards (proving the superstition's worth!).

THE PLAYOFF BEARD REACHES THE OWNER'S BOX

The playoff beard has pretty much been a players-only tradition, but a new era began in 2008–09 when Pittsburgh Penguins owner Mario Lemieux adopted the superstition along with the team. This isn't surprising given that Lemieux was (a) a Hall of Fame player himself and (b) landlord to the team's captain, Sidney Crosby. No doubt at the start of the playoffs, over a bowl of cereal at breakfast, the captain challenged the owner to play along and toss the razor aside for the duration. And so it was that on the ice and in the dressing room after Pittsburgh's historic victory in June 2009, Lemieux raised the Cup high above his bearded face in triumph. It is highly doubtful that the older and more corporate owners will follow Mario's lead, but Penguins fans can be sure that Lemieux will continue with the tradition as long as it has strength (having Crosby and Evgeni Malkin on the team doesn't hurt, either).

TO LIFT OR ONLY TO SMILE?

Probably the most inconsistent superstition in the NHL concerns the tactile fortunes of the Prince of Wales Trophy (awarded to the Eastern Conference champions) and the Clarence Campbell Bowl (awarded to the Western Conference champions), two beautiful examples of silverware that have done nothing to deserve the plague-like misfortunes that have befallen them. Sometimes.

Each trophy is presented to the winning team after it claims the conference title and, by so doing, earns a spot in the Stanley Cup finals. The problem is that—as some players and teams would have fans believe—to hoist these trophies is to accept and celebrate mediocrity. It's as much as saying, "Yeah! We've won the conference title!" But, of course, being one of the *two* best teams in the league is meaningless compared to winning the Stanley Cup itself, so players often eschew lifting the trophy as a way of saying, "This means little to us. The only trophy we're lifting is the Stanley Cup."

The on-ice presentation started within the last two decades, so it doesn't have the history of the Cup presentation or even the playoff beard. And the league itself admits that the two conference trophies aren't as important because these are presented by Bill Daly, the right-hand man of NHL commissioner Gary Bettman. It is Bettman himself, of course, who delivers the Stanley Cup to the winning captain.

As for the players, there are three kinds of presentation reaction. First, the player can actually accept and lift the trophy from the presentation table. Second, the polite thanks-but-no-thanks reaction is to smile and gently touch the trophy as it sits on said table. And third, the player stands beside the table without so much as acknowledging the presence of any silverware.

New Jersey captain Scott Stevens had no problem with lifting the Prince of Wales, and he led the Devils to three Stanley Cups. Ditto for Steve Yzerman and

Nicklas Lidstrom in the Western Conference with Detroit. But in 2008, Sidney Crosby refused to touch the Prince of Wales, and the Penguins went on to lose to Detroit in the Cup finals. In 2009, Crosby sought to reverse his fortunes, so he lifted the trophy (but not overhead) and his team went on to win the Cup.

In short, these two conference trophies elicit a superstition of some form every year, and every year the trophy is either touched or not touched, resulting in either victory or loss of the Stanley Cup. In other words, go figure.

DON'T TOUCH STANLEY UNLESS YOU'VE EARNED THE RIGHT

Touching trophies is never more contentious than with the Stanley Cup itself. This is also a modern superstition because in the old days players on the winning team got to take the trophy into the dressing room after the game and nothing more. The league took the trophy back to the NHL offices in Montreal the next day, and the sacred Cup sat in a small safe until the following year, when it was again hauled out for a couple days.

But in 1993, the NHL started to allow each player and staff member of the winning team to have a day with the Cup. The team kept it for several days after winning it, culminating in the Cup parade through the downtown city streets (or, in the case of New Jersey, the arena parking lot), and throughout the summer players have taken it to towns, hospitals, golf courses, and mountaintops all over the world.

However, the more Stanley travels, the more he is exposed for the world to touch and enjoy and be photographed with. For any serious hockey player, though, the rule is very simple. If you touch the Cup before having won it, forget it—you never will.

This superstition was painfully observed by Jordan Staal and his brothers Marc and Jared. The incredible Staal family consists of four brothers. Eric plays for the Carolina Hurricanes; Jordan is with the Pittsburgh Penguins; Marc is with the New York Rangers; and, the baby, Jared, is on the road to the NHL.

In 2002, Eric, the eldest, helped the Hurricanes to a surprise Cup victory in his rookie season, and, of course, in the summer he took the Cup back to the family farm. The other brothers, all with their eyes on the same prize at some point down the road, had to be very careful. They were in awe of their big brother for winning the Cup, but they didn't want to get carried away and jinx their own chances of winning it. So they celebrated with Eric, from a distance.

CHANGE OF NUMBERS, CHANGE OF LUCK

Most NHL players have a lucky number or choose a sweater number for a particular reason. In Sidney Crosby's case, for instance, his 87 represents both the date and month of his birth (August 7) as well as his year of birth (1987). Alexander Ovechkin wears number 8 because that was his mother's number when she played basketball at the Olympics.

Generally speaking, once a player makes the NHL wearing a particular number, he feels it gives him luck and wants to keep it. But when he is traded, complications arise. Often someone else is wearing his number on the team he has been traded to. Players overcome this obstacle by several means. The easiest is that, if he is a big enough star, the incumbent on the new team will simply surrender the digit out of respect. Failing that, the incoming player can offer a cash incentive.

Or, the traded player can become creative. When Scott Gomez—always number 19—signed with Montreal in the summer of 2009, he did so knowing that number 19 was in the rafters for Larry Robinson. Gomez merely flipped the digits and wore number 91. When Phil Esposito was traded from Boston to the Rangers, Rod Gilbert had number 7, so "Espo" doubled the digit and wore number 77. This is also how Wayne Gretzky got from his favoured number 9 (in honour of his hero, Gordie Howe) to 99; when Wayne arrived in Sault Ste. Marie for his first year of junior hockey, number 9 was taken, so he doubled it to produce 99.

Perhaps the most egregious form of succoring the greater talent happened in Vancouver when Mark Messier signed as a free agent. He had had number 11 his whole career, but that number was unofficially retired by the Canucks in honour of Wayne Maki. The Canucks, without consulting the Maki family, simply gave the number to Messier, who accepted it without much moral dilemma. Coincidence or not, the Canucks never even qualified for the playoffs during Messier's three years with the team, and after his departure no one wore number 11 ever again.

Of course, some players simply switch numbers when they get to a new team to change their luck. After all, being traded is not a form of flattery, so playing in a new city might well merit a new number. Still other players change their number for simple good luck. Joe Thornton wore number 6 with Boston for a while, but it simply "didn't feel right." He went to number 19, and he turned into one of the top players in the league.

Perhaps the greatest example of a number change, though, is Maurice Richard's switcheroo from number

15 to 9. In 1940–41, his last year in the senior league, with Quebec, he broke his ankle during the first game of the season. The next year, he broke it again after just sixteen NHL games with the Canadiens. The summer of 1943, though, his first daughter was born. Huguette weighed nine pounds, and to celebrate her birth and to try to change his fortunes on ice he changed to number 9 for the upcoming season. The rest, as they say, is history.

STICKS: THE WAND IS PURE MAGIC

More than any other piece of equipment or facet of the game, the stick is what players fret over most. Whether hard-working defensive defencemen or top scorers in the league, they are most consumed by their stick. It is the instrument most players connect to success or failure. Indeed, on off-days an NHL dressing room can be crowded with stick reps from various companies meeting with players and fine-tuning the stick to a player's specifications. Once these sticks are crafted into a perfect style, the player has his own "pattern," as it is called, which is then sold across the country to the average Joe playing shinny with friends.

The stick has many nicknames: twig, cue, and

lumber among them. But the crafting of one to a player's needs can be complex. The shaft can be heavy or light, stiff or flexible. The lie can be high or low; the blade straight or curved. The stick can be made of wood, graphite, or a composite. It can be one piece or two. And, of course, there is the intangible "feel" that a player can't describe or design or write down on a piece of paper.

Once the player receives a batch of sticks, he then fine-tunes them even more. He'll shave the top and wrap tape around the knob in a particular way. He'll blow-torch the blade a bit here and there, or shave the toe. But once he finally has the stick in game-ready shape, it becomes alive, almost like a brother or lover. The hard work is done, but the loving is still required to make it perform.

Literally every player has a superstition associated with his stick, but here is a generous sample of what various players past and present have done with their most prized possession:

- Daniel Brière talks to his stick.
- Vincent Lecavalier won't let his stick touch the ground.
- Pierre Mondou carved the letter G on all of his sticks for luck, the G standing both for *goals* and *gagner* (win).

- Joe Nieuwendyk sprinkled baby powder on the blade of his sticks before each game.
- Stéphane Richer made sure that his number 10 was stamped on all of his sticks.
- Petr Svoboda would put his stick in the same place during intermission and wouldn't let anyone else touch it.
- Darryl Sydor always liked to lean his stick up against the same black scuff mark on the wall. One time, the arena crew painted that wall, covering the spot. The next day, Sydor remade the scuff mark in the same place.
- John Tavares gets five sticks ready the day before a game. He puts four at his stall and a fifth near the skate sharpener.
- Darcy Tucker prepares only one stick per game because he believes the others might get jealous.

PYRAMID POWER

Strange doesn't begin to explain the connection between the King's Chamber of the Great Pyramid of Egypt and the 1976 Stanley Cup playoffs, but there is a connection all the same. Toronto and Philadelphia faced each other in the playoffs three successive years, from 1974 to 1976. These were

Toronto coach Red Kelly tried unsuccessfully to use Pyramid Power to help the Leafs defeat the Flyers in the playoffs.

violent series full of fighting, animosity, and bitter rivalry, but in the end the Flyers won the first two series and went on to win the Stanley Cup. In 1976, though, Leafs coach Red Kelly tried to get those ancient Egyptians on board through Pyramid Power.

Kelly's sons had recently visited Egypt and had told their dad about the reputed mythical, mystical effects of pyramids. Pyramids were supposed to allow food to remain fresh longer, keep razor blades sharp, increase sexual performance and prowess, and even provide energy beyond human capacity. None of this had ever been proved, of course, but it was worth a try for Kelly, so he outfitted the Leafs' dressing room and players' bench with small pyramids perhaps about a foot wide at the base.

The superstition was threefold. First, it was a way of uniting the team. Second, it was a way, he hoped, of psyching out the enemy Flyers. Third, it was a way of motivating the team, making them believe in themselves as somehow gifted or blessed with a power the other team didn't have. The frenzy in Toronto during the series was exceptional, but in the end the Flyers won game seven, on home ice, 7–3, thanks to another superstition—Kate Smith.

KATE SMITH

Superstitions are often just habits couched as something more important, ways of doing things that are about comfort more than guaranteeing success. But if there ever was a genuine superstition that had some teeth to it, something that one might actually say worked because it was a superstition, then Kate

Smith singing "God Bless America" at Philadelphia Flyers home games was it.

The tradition began inauspiciously on December 11, 1969, at the behest of Flyers vice-president Lou Scheinfield. He insisted a song other than the "Star-Spangled Banner" be played before the game, and Kate Smith's recording of "God Bless America" was deemed best in the Spectrum. The Flyers beat Toronto that night, 6–3, and the legend began. It wasn't until the home opener of the 1973–74 season started that Smith first performed the song live, resulting in another win over the Leafs, this a 2–0 gem.

Of course, the trick to such a superstition was to pick and choose games at which the song would appear. After all, if the team played it for every home game, the mystique would be shattered because no team wins every home game over the course of a season. That being said, Scheinfield didn't pad the superstition by playing the song for weak teams at unimportant times. Indeed, Smith's rendition was reserved for key playoff games or games against top rivals.

Smith's health began to fade by the late 1970s and she passed away in 1986. The song was played less frequently during these years, and there were many years when it wasn't played at all. However, in a new arena in the twenty-first century, Smith's voice

Kate Smith's singing of "God Bless America" had a very real good-luck effect on the Philadelphia Flyers in the 1970s and beyond.

has made a comeback, thanks to the fancy score-boards above centre ice. In 2007–08, for instance, the song was played nine times, and the Flyers had a very impressive 7–2–0 record in those games.

In all, Smith's "God Bless America" has been played 102 times since that first occasion in 1969. Through all those years and roster changes and new opponents, the Flyers have an astounding 87–23–4 record. Not perfect, not a guaranteed win, but for a superstition, it's pretty good. And for good luck and good measure, the Flyers recently unveiled a large bronze statue of Smith outside their arena so her memory, and fortuitous presence, would live on forever.

DON'T FOLLOW DEATH

There is a superstition that is never spoken in so many words but that exists all the same. In a nutshell, players never wear the number of a player who has died during his career. There have been several instances of this, and in each case there is a double meaning of superstition and respect.

Take the case of Steve Chiasson, for instance. The Carolina Hurricanes defenceman died after he crashed his truck while drunk late on the night of May 3, 1999. A solid if unspectacular player, Chiasson had not had the kind of career that called for retiring his number, and his death was entirely self-inflicted. The Hurricanes have never officially retired his number 3, but no player has worn it since and it is understood that no one will.

Going back a little farther, Pelle Lindbergh crashed his car into a wall while driving drunk on November 10, 1985. At the height of his career, with Philadelphia, the Flyers chose not to retire his number 31 (in part because he hadn't been a star for very long; in part because of the way he died), but no Flyers player has worn Lindbergh's 31 since.

Sensational Pittsburgh Penguins rookie Michel Brière also died after a car accident. He remained in a coma for eleven months before succumbing to his head injuries in 1971, and it wasn't until 2001 that his number 21 was officially raised to the rafters of the Igloo. However, no Penguins player ever wore number 21 after his accident. He had been a promising youngster but had played only one full season with the team.

Dan Snyder has been similarly honoured by the Atlanta Thrashers since dying as a result of injuries suffered while being a passenger in a car driven recklessly by teammate Dany Heatley on October 5, 2003. Snyder was only at the start of a promising career, but his number 42 has been in official retirement ever since.

The protocol is very simple. Any player who has had an outstanding career with a team or has made a great contribution to, or had a great impact on, a team will have his number retired if he dies during his career. But any player who doesn't have the same outstanding career but suffers a fatal injury will likely have his number unofficially retired in that the team will simply never issue it again. And players, being superstitious, would never want to wear a number that bestowed death upon its last wearer. Sounds a bit cruel and creepy perhaps, but it's a deeply ingrained superstition all the same.

DETROIT'S OCTOPUS

It all began in 1952 when the NHL playoffs were a mere two rounds of best-of-seven and a team needed only eight victories to claim the silver bowl. Detroit was at the height of its powers, led by the dynamic duo of Gordie Howe and Ted Lindsay, backed by goalie Terry Sawchuk, and loaded with plenty of talent up front and on defence.

As a measure of good luck, Peter Cusimano, an owner of a local fish market in the Motor City, tossed an octopus on the ice at the start of game one of the Detroit–Toronto playoff series. An octopus had eight limbs, and the animal served as good luck for the Red Wings' playoff run. The team went on to sweep the Maple Leafs in the semi-finals and Montreal in the finals to win the Cup, and the legend of the octopus began.

The superstition of the playoff octopus toss has continued to this day, although the NHL tried to snuff the tradition out several years ago in connection with the rat tossing in Florida that began in 1996. Panthers fans were tossing plastic rodents onto the ice after every goal because the team's captain, Scott Mellanby, had found and killed a rat in the team's dressing room. The problem was, however, that the rat-tossing celebrations got out of control. Fans started to toss the rats onto the ice after each and every goal in the playoffs, and then so many fans tossed so many thousands of the critters that the game was delayed several minutes each time.

The NHL instituted a rule whereby the home team would be penalized two minutes for delay of game because of such antics, and the rat tossing stopped. But Detroit fans realized they, too, could hurt their team if an octopus cleanup constituted a delay of game. So, for a short while, until the rat tossing had quelled, the octopi enjoyed a stay of execution in Detroit. But the superstition has found renewed life and flourishes as fans have discovered referees' reluctance to penalize the home team now that the rat tossing has been eliminated.

Detroit has been the most successful team in the NHL over the last decade, so anyone wanting to see the toss in person need only attend a playoff game at the Joe Louis Arena.

CRAPPIEST SUPERSTITION EVER

Fortunately, some superstitions have a short shelf life, but for a few weeks in the spring of 1975, the New York Islanders had the smelliest superstition known to hockey.

These were the days when the first round of the playoffs, called the Preliminary Round, consisted of a short best-of-three series. The Islanders and Rangers met in this round in 1975, but Madison Square Garden was also hosting the circus on off-nights. One night, friend of the Islanders' Billy Harris collected a generous sample of elephant dung and put it in an appropriate bag as a good-luck charm for the team. Unfortunately, it worked. The Islanders, in only their third year of existence, scored in overtime of game three to eliminate the "Broadway Blueshirts" and advance to the quarter-finals against Pittsburgh.

That series seemed to mark the end of the dung's effectiveness, though. The Penguins won the first three games of the best-of-seven series and were well on their way to the semi-finals. But the Islanders kept carrying the dung around and the team won game four by a 3–1 score to avoid being swept and forcing a fifth game. They won that, 4–2, and won again in game six, 4–1, to force a deciding game.

Even still, there was no way the Penguins could lose. The only other team to win a series after trail-ing 3–0 was the Maple Leafs, and that was back in the finals of 1942 against Detroit. Lo and behold, "Chico" Resch played shutout hockey, and Ed Westfall scored the only goal of the game with five minutes left in the third period to give the Islanders a 4–3 series win and a place in history.

They were on to the semi-finals—bag of dung in hand, needless to say—to face Philadelphia. Again the Islanders lost the first three games, but they hauled the dung along and won games four, five, and six, an absolutely extraordinary comeback for the second straight series. The Flyers, however, would not go down in infamy as did the Penguins, and Philly won game seven, 4–1, sending the dung to the recycling bin of crazy superstitions.

Said Dave Lewis, a member of the olfactory-challenged team: "We had that Madison Square Garden aroma around us all the time from when we beat the Rangers. And you thought playoff beards were weird? Our poor trainers!"

STAN THE MAN

Stan Weir had a perfectly respectable 642-game stint in the NHL. He began his career in 1972 with the hapless California Golden Seals, then played for Toronto before joining the Edmonton Oilers just as they were starting to dominate. Weir was traded to Colorado during the 1981–82 season, however, so he was never part of the Oilers dynasty that won four Cups in five years in the mid-1980s. But Weir returned to the Oilers, in a manner of speaking, and helped the team win in the 2006 playoffs and beyond.

His resurrection can be credited to one Allan Mitchell, an ad salesperson with an Edmonton radio station who also ran his own popular Oilers blog called Lowetide (in reference to former player, later general manager, and now team president Kevin Lowe).

Mitchell would post photos of Oilers alumni on

his site, and it seemed that whenever he posted a picture of Weir, the Oilers won. Between 2006 and 2008, Mitchell published the Weir photo sixteen times, and the Oilers had a remarkable 12–4 record in those games. The Oil didn't make it into the 2009 or 2010 playoffs, so Weir's run ended there. Still, it seems that the hard-working Weir, who had his only two thirty-goal seasons with the Oilers, has had good success as a beacon of superstition for the team. No doubt, once the team returns to the post-season, he'll be there on Lowetide, smiling the faded smile of an alumnus gone but by no means forgotten.

THE NET IS SACRED

A team defends its goal with every ounce of pride and fight it can muster. Sometimes it does so perfectly and wins by a shutout; sometimes it does so less perfectly but still wins. Other times, of course, the other team does the same. But there is one very important unwritten rule in hockey's code that is never violated without punishment—scoring (or trying to score) into the team's goal at any other time than during play.

The most common example occurs when the whistle is blown just as a player is about to shoot the puck. A smart player will let up and not release the shot. A disturber will let a shot go anyway, at which point the defending team will charge at him and demand an explanation.

Another occurrence happens when a delayed penalty is in progress and one team has an empty net and a sixth attacker on the ice. When the defending team gains possession of the puck, the whistle goes and the penalty is assessed, but heaven forbid if this possession takes place near the vacated goal and the defending player casually smacks the puck into the open net. Again, he'll be immediately accosted by his opponents with vehemence.

In the 1970s and 1980s, bench-clearing brawls ensued from another form of empty-net goal. The pre-game warm-up is a time to get ready for the game, of course, but it's also a time for psychological preparation. Players require differing lengths of time to prepare, and many are superstitious about being the last off the ice or the last to score a goal on their own empty net. It's a way of setting a positive tone for the rest of the game. Get a final goal during warm-up; get a goal during the game.

However, it is absolutely forbidden to shoot the puck down the ice into the other team's empty net at the end of warm-up. The centre red line is the battle line during this preparation, and no player or puck is allowed to cross that threshold without repercussions.

The games that went on to prevent such a tactic were incredible. Like some sort of elimination contest, one player after another would fire a puck into his net and skate off, eventually whittling that number down to one or two a side. Sometimes players on the home team felt it was their right to fire a puck the length of the ice into the other team's empty net, for good luck. Oftentimes, if the player missed the long shot, the fans would boo, knowing this presaged misfortune for the game itself.

But during the playoffs, all bets were off, and visiting players would guard their net until the home team's last player was off the ice. If the player showed no signs of leaving, the opponent would turn the net around and push it against the end boards, preventing a long shot from going in. Home fans also booed this tactic. Sometimes an opponent would fire the puck into the home team's net after the last player had left the ice, but that player would be watching from the corridor. Upon seeing this, he'd skate back onto the ice and challenge the player.

Bench-clearing brawls sometimes resulted, but slowly, over time, this empty-net goal tactic faded in importance, and all teams now mutually agree simply never to fire the puck into the other team's goal at the end of warm-up. Some superstitions die hard, but this one was murder to keep alive.

THE MARCH TO WAR

It is a superstition so old, so ingrained in the consciousness of players and fans that it hardly seems like a superstition at all. It's not even a custom or habit or formality. It's just part of the game, like the puck, boards, and net. It is the team's march to the ice to begin every game and period.

Of course, players being players, a team can't simply skate out to the ice to begin a game. There must be a reason, a logic, a determining process and order to this march from the dressing room to the playing surface. And so, for as long as anyone can remember, it is the starting goalie who goes on the ice first. Why? Simple. He's the most important player on the team. Without a good game from him, you'll lose. That's why he wears number 1 (okay, this tradition barely survives, but still . . .). There may be twelve forwards and six or seven defencemen in a game, but there's only one goalie.

It doesn't stop there. Teams have a specific order of every player following the goalie, an order that begins from the time they leave the dressing room.

It is a calculated order, based on superstition, seniority, or some other frivolous factor. Oftentimes the captain will be the last player on the ice, but not always. Sometimes he's the second player, after the goalie, the second most important player on the team, as it were.

Perhaps the most unusual and symmetrical order belongs to Team USA's women. No one knows when, why, or how it started, but for several years now the women march onto the ice in numerical order. Number 1 goes first, then 2, 3, 4, and up to the highest number. It is a marvel of precision to watch, an order created by players with a mathematical penchant for preciseness. No other team has such a numeric ritual.

In the NHL, for instance, the marching order is upset every time a player is demoted or traded and new players arrive. They must fit into the order somewhere, somehow. With Team USA's women, though, old players and new are part of the same numbered sequence.

LAST TAPS

Think of the ice as a war zone. The walk from the dressing room to the ice is the walk of soldiers going to war. In between are the final moments of peace, the moments for reflection, prayer, and focus, as they concentrate on what lies ahead. As they skate around the ice to limber up one final time before the national anthem, players finish at the goal crease, where they congregate around their most important player, the one who is likely to make the difference between victory and defeat—the goalie.

The purpose is simple—to wish the goalie good luck. But each player has his own little ritual, and the team as a whole has a superstitious pattern to this process. One player will tap only the goalie's pads; another will rub his mask or smack the posts; still another will speak certain words. Always there is one last player who stands beside the goalie throughout this process, the player who has to be the last to offer his good-luck wishes.

This is the NHL way. In women's hockey, in junior leagues, and in American college hockey, the usual routine is to huddle around the goalie en masse, a superstition made spectacle by the high shot above the net captured by television cameras. Everyone cuddles close, bows heads, and repeats a chant or mantra, or the captain might say a few special words to inveigh a great performance from the group.

And then, all but the starters head to the players' bench and the game begins. They have done all that they can do before the opening faceoff.

A MAGICAL FEW WEEKS

The season was 1950–51, and the New York Rangers were off to a miserable start. By early December, the "Broadway Blueshirts" were already in danger of falling too far out of the playoff race. They needed something. They needed . . . a miracle.

Enter restaurateur Gene Leone, a Rangers fan with a slant for promotion. He decided to concoct a mixture from his kitchen, with some red wine for flavour, and give it to the Rangers for a little extra oomph before games. He called it Leone's Magic Elixir. Desperate, the Rangers bought into it, and— incredibly—the team started to win!

Early in the new year they enjoyed a lengthy winning streak, but their big test came in January when they visited Toronto to play at Maple Leaf Gardens, a stop that had been unkind to the team for many years. By now, everyone knew about the magic drink, and Leafs owner Conn Smythe made plans with Canada Customs officers to confiscate the elixir as the players crossed the border.

The Rangers managed to get the elixir across anyway, and staff drove like madmen to the Gardens to administer the potion to the players. It worked. The Rangers won the game, 4–2, and continued to play well for a while longer. An NHL season, though, was seventy games in those days, a very long time to keep a magic potion working wonders. Indeed, by season's end, the Rangers were in fifth place and out of the playoffs, but for a wonderful few weeks they had an *Awakenings* experience and played, well, out of their minds.

THE MASCOT

Take a look at the team photo of the 1911–12 Quebec Bulldogs. Playing in the National Hockey Association, precursor to the NHL, the team finished in first place to win the Stanley Cup, ahead of the Ottawa Senators, Montreal Wanderers, and Montreal Canadiens. The Bulldogs then beat the Moncton Victorias in a two-game series, winning both games by 9–3 and 8–0 scores. The team was led by the great scoring star Joe Malone, but front and centre in that photo is . . . a bulldog.

The dog was the team's mascot, and as such was one of hockey's first, but not last, good-luck charms. The Bulldogs won the Cup again the next year, and right in the middle is, once again, the dog. His luck ran out after that, but teams routinely had mascots of one sort or another.

When the Leafs won the Stanley Cup in 1942,

The Quebec Bulldogs won the Stanley Cup for the 1911-12 season with a bulldog mascot, featured front and centre in the team picture.

Hugh Smythe, the son of the team's owner, Conn Smythe, was listed on the Cup engraving as the team's mascot. Little Hugh did nothing but hang around the dressing room, grab sticks for the players, and be the team owner's rink-rat son, but he was also considered the Leafs' good-luck charm. He got his name on the Cup for so little—and so much.

ORDER OF DRESS

Every player does it. Every player acknowledges its importance. So how can this be a superstition? Isn't it just a habit? No.

Ask any player and he'll tell you he dresses either left-right or right-left. That is, he puts on left shin pad, right shin pad. Left elbow pad, right. Left skate, right. Everything left to right (or right to left).

What's interesting about this superstition is that it is unalterable. When they are in a slump, players will change sticks, sweater numbers, skates even, but they won't ever change the order of getting dressed. Putting equipment on is the fundamental first step of playing the game. Each player has his own method, and each method started when he was a small boy. That is the superstition of getting dressed in a particular way.

That comfort and familiarity, that childhood reference point, allows the player to relax. It gives him the confidence that he knows what he's doing because he's done it countless times before. It makes him comfortable because it's something he can do by rote, without thinking. Anyone who has ever tied a skate too tight or tightened an elbow pad too much knows how uncomfortable equipment can be.

To change the order of getting dressed almost

feels like wearing someone else's equipment. It feels strange to put on the right skate first if you've always put on the left one first. And strange is not a good feeling for a hockey player. Familiar is what he wants. He wants his equipment to feel like house clothes. Guy Lafleur used to say he felt his skates were like slippers. Bobby Orr always went barefoot when playing (as did countless kids of the next generation, trying to emulate the great number 4).

In the end, the superstition can be boiled down to this. By dressing in a particular way, a player feels the most comfortable, and this, in turn, will allow him to play his best. That is the essence of all superstitions.

A GOOD COB

The word *cob* is used in hockey to describe a shutout, the corn on the cob resembling a big zero, as it were. A team that wins 4–0, say, wins the game "four cob."

But cob has another positive superstition attached to it, thanks to the Ottawa Nationals of the World Hockey Association during the league's inaugural season. The end of the 1972–73 schedule was shaping up to be a disaster for the team and a playoff spot was a distant hope at best. But before a game against the Alberta (later to be Edmonton) Oilers on February 25, 1973, Nationals trainer Peter Unwin found a half-eaten cob of corn in the corridor outside the team's dressing room.

Unwin picked up the odd discard and tossed it to Gavin Kirk, telling him it was a good-luck charm. Kirk kept it at his stall for no particular reason, but that night the Nationals beat the Oilers, thanks to a lucky goal. Before their next game, against Cleveland, Kirk had a special ceremony all ready. He had kept the cob tucked inside one of his gloves. Before going onto the ice, he removed it, got six players to touch it, and then took one kernel from the cob and tossed it to teammate Ken Stephanson.

Kirk and the Nationals used this ritual for twelve of the team's final thirteen regular season games, winning every time. Their only loss, to Los Angeles, happened when they didn't perform their superstitious ritual. The team made it into the playoffs despite losing the final two games of the regular season.

That's where the cob-ian luck ended. They lost 4–1 to the New England Whalers in the first round of the playoffs, and Kirk sent the cob whence it came, to the trash.

THE LUCKY LOONIE

They call Dan Craig "The Ice Man" because as the man in charge of maintaining the ice at Northlands Coliseum in Edmonton he has long been known to produce the best sheet hockey players can find. And so there was no question that in the time leading up to the 2002 Olympic Winter Games in Salt Lake City, Utah, Craig would be the man in charge. Logically, he hired his Edmonton crew to join him to produce the Olympic ice, but one of their number, Trent Evans, went above and beyond the call of duty for his country.

Evans buried a one-dollar Canadian coin, affectionately known as a loonie, under centre ice as a good-luck charm for the men's and women's teams. He told the players of his scheming in the hopes the loonie would offset any "home-ice (i.e., psychological) advantage" the Americans might have had from playing in their own backyard, as it were.

For his own satisfaction, Evans also put a dime under the loonie. On February 21, 2002, the Canadian women defeated the American team, 3–2, to win gold, and during their celebrations several bent down to kiss the centre-ice spot under which the loonie lay.

Three days later, the men also beat the USA, 5–2, to win gold, after which team general manager

Wayne Gretzky scraped the loonie out from the ice and presented it to the Hockey Hall of Fame. Evans claimed the dime as his own and has kept it among his prized possessions ever since. Of course, the IOC was not thrilled with the patriotic gesture, and four years later Craig was again supervisor in Turin, but there was no sign of Evans.

Nevertheless, the lucky loonie spawned many a sequel. Team Canada used it again at the 2003 World Championship, which the Canadians won on an Anson Carter goal in overtime. This coin was taped inside the Swedish net by Canadian officials before the gold-medal game.

The superstition became so popular that the Royal Canadian Mint even issued a special lucky loonie coin in time for Turin (2006) and Vancouver (2010), but the magical coin that gave the men their first gold in half a century in 2002 remains the pinnacle of superstitious coins.

Amazingly, there was no such lucky loonie necessary in Vancouver in February 2010, yet both the men's and women's teams managed to duplicate their feat of eight years ago, winning gold against the Americans.

EAT RIGHT

From a hockey player's perspective, hockey games take place at an awkward time. When the faceoff occurs at 7:30 p.m., say, it throws his whole eating routine out of whack. Ergo, hockey players have their pre-game meals much earlier in the day, then relax and sleep, and have another meal after the game.

As science has evolved and we learn more about the benefits of certain foods, this vital pre-game meal has changed significantly. For decades it was considered sacred to have a steak with vegetables as the big meal at about noon, before a nap and the game.

In the last twenty years or so, players have shifted to a high-carb diet for extra energy. As a result, most favour a plate of pasta. The Rangers' Sean Avery acknowledged as much when asked about his game-day routine. "We all eat the same thing before games," he said. "For me, it's spaghetti and chicken. Every game. My whole life. Since I was nine years old."

Indeed, the meal is essential for playing well, so in this case superstition and common sense merge. The meal is part of that pre-game routine, but if a player is used to one thing, and if that meal has helped get him to the NHL, he isn't likely to change. Also, a player's stomach must be understood and coddled. It's not possible to play one's best with indigestion or other gastrointestinal difficulty. Pasta, chicken, and vegetables are all easy to eat and digest, and they are filling enough and provide enough nutrients to be a perfect repast.

Few players have had their diet dissected so much as Doug Gilmour of the Toronto Maple Leafs during the 1993 and 1994 playoffs. Blessed with the heart of a lion, Gilmour was never the biggest or strongest player in the league, yet his Herculean efforts in those two playoffs almost propelled Toronto to its first Stanley Cup finals appearance since 1967.

The gruelling playoff schedule, the extra minutes played, and the pressure and intensity all wore away at "Dougie." Yet one game after another he endured and starred for the team, crediting pasta for his strength. In his case, the key was not one large game-day lunch. Rather, it was seven or eight small meals of spaghetti throughout the day to keep his stomach less than completely full but his energy level always high.

A COACH'S TIE

Players can afford the luxury of superstitions because anything that might improve their performance by

1 per cent or 100 per cent is worth trying. As well, their performance can either confirm the quality and power of a superstition or it can supersede or negate a superstition. In other words, what happens on the ice is the ultimate test of anything they do in the name of good luck.

But they aren't the only ones who are superstitious. Coaches, for instance, have their routines and lucky habits, such as wearing a lucky tie for big games. In the case of Detroit Red Wings coach Mike Babcock, his lucky tie is one bearing the design of McGill University in Montreal, his alma mater, where he played for the Redmen for four years (1983–87). He first wore it in 2007, as a gesture of respect to McGill.

It is a strange and serendipitous choice, in some respects, however, because the logo on the Detroit sweater comes from the Winged Wheelers of Montreal. Babcock was completing the circle by returning to Montreal (via McGill) for good luck, and it worked more often than not.

Babcock knows that his lucky tie will have greater lasting power if he picks and chooses when to wear it. He focuses on the playoffs, of course, and the fact that the tie helped him get to the Stanley Cup finals in both 2008 and 2009 is a testament to both its powers and his strategy. In 2008, he won

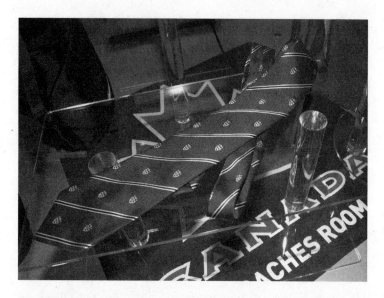

Coach Mike Babcock donated his lucky McGill tie to the Hockey Hall of Fame after leading Canada's men to gold at the Vancouver Olympics.

four times and had only one loss with the tie, in game five of the finals when Pittsburgh won in overtime. But he usually wears ties based on an even more important superstition. He prefers to wear a tie selected by his daughter.

Such was not the case, however, during the Vancouver Olympics when he coached Team Canada. In a preliminary-round game against the United States, he didn't wear his McGill tie and Canada lost, 5–3. The rematch, the most anticipated Olympic hockey game ever played and one watched by some 26.5 million Canadians, saw Babcock return to his lucky tie. Of course, Canada won the gold medal thanks to a Sidney Crosby overtime goal, 3–2.

Babcock's coaching life is dictated by more than just ties. "I'm a smart-enough guy to know superstition doesn't matter, but I still do some superstitious things," he once confided. "I polish my shoes all the time the exact same way because I've done it for years. When I fill out the lineup card, I always wait till I get the other team's. Little dumb things that . . . don't affect the outcome, but when you're trying to control the uncontrollable, you'll do anything."

Scotty Bowman was famous for being tie superstitious, often wearing the same one every night during a team's winning streak, changing after a loss. More recently, another Montreal coach had success with a tie. Guy Carbonneau was given Hermès neckwear by his wife, Line, on March 18, 2008, on his forty-eighth birthday. A week later, he wore it for a game against Ottawa, which the Canadiens won, 7–5, to clinch a playoff spot. He wore it for the first and last game against Boston in the first round of the playoffs, both victories, and by this time the neckwear had become famous. It had a Facebook group set up by fans, and one Montreal newspaper provided a cut-out version for fans to wear to games.

Carbonneau brought it out for a fifth time for game five of the Conference semi-finals against Philadelphia, but the team was trailing 3–1 in the series and lost the final game, 6–4, to end Carbonneau's tie success. "Am I superstitious?" he asked rhetorically when asked about the power of the tie. "Yes, a little. I think we all are. As the play-offs go on, you become more superstitious. All the little things become more important, not only individually, but with the team as well."

THAT'S NOT A RUG

Starting in the early 1990s, every NHL team up-graded their arena, ditching the small, comfortable barn in favour of the gargantuan palace with hundreds of private boxes, acres of concession stands, and improved amenities. But nothing changed more during the construction than the home team's dressing room, which went from being a place to put on equipment to a vast tract of land with plush carpet, kitchen, weight room, medical centre, a veritable equipment outlet that would rival the largest retail establishments, the whole shebang, and then some.

As a result, the actual dressing room became only one small section of the players' area, and this, too, was outfitted with the biggest and best. In the middle of this room is always a large, round rug displaying the team logo. Being right in the middle, of course, it longs to be stepped on as the easiest way to get from point A to point B in a straight line, but team constitution forbids any feet from sullying the logo. It represents the goal, the focal point, the spot in the middle of the room where every player from every stall can see the significance of his endeavour. This is also the room reporters enter to interview players for post-game comments, and in every arena the home team has staff to guide these interlopers away from the logo.

A famous myth concerning the 2002 Olympic gold-medal game between the women's teams of Canada and the United States had it that the Americans had a Canadian logo in the centre of their room and stepped on it repeatedly to indicate lack of respect, lack of intimidation. No American player ever confirmed the report—and it is very likely untrue—but it does indicate the importance of the logo in the middle of the dressing room. Look, admire, be awed—but tread not.

THE LUCKY BUTT OF L.A.

Thankfully, some superstitions are just not meant to last, and the "Lucky Butt" is one such specimen. There was a radio host from the *Mark and Brian* show on KLOS FM 95.5 in Los Angeles who sat on the pitching mound in Oakland before an A's game at the 1988 World Series against the Dodgers. Los Angeles won the series, and the legend of "Lucky Butt" was born.

Flash-forward a year when the Los Angeles Kings and Edmonton Oilers hooked up in the 1989 playoffs. The Oilers took a commanding 3–1 lead in the series, and that's when the big butt man stepped in. He sat on the Los Angeles Forum ice with exposed posterior before game five, and the Kings produced a dramatic 4–2 win to stay alive.

Not wanting to mess with success, "Lucky Butt" flew to Edmonton for game six, sat on the Northlands Coliseum ice with his bare butt, and the Kings again won, 4–1, to force a decisive game seven back in La-La Land. Wouldn't you know it, but another frozen butt moment helped the Kings win the game, 6–3, and the series, 4–3, but the charm wasn't as effective in the next round when the Kings faced the Calgary Flames.

"Lucky Butt" tried to do his thing, but the Flames

were simply a great hockey team and swept the Kings in four games. "Lucky Butt"'s day in the sun was done.

REFEREES ARE PEOPLE, TOO

Players aren't the only ones on the ice, and they're not the only ones expected to perform to the best of their ability. The pace and quality of the game is often dictated by the quality of the officiating, and referees also have to prepare if they are to be at their best.

The officiating crew always arrives at the arena as a group, with security, and they all do various things to prepare for a game. They skate more than any player all night, so they have to stretch, work out the kinks, and be mentally ready for anything. Like players, they also have a game-day meal in the early afternoon, followed by a nap.

They also dress left to right or right to left, as they have all of their career, but they don't have sticks and don't have as much opportunity to be superstitious. Their job is to perform so well that the fans don't even know they're out there.

In the days before Plexiglas, when there was fencing that extended only in each zone not even to the blue lines, referees were very superstitious about one thing in particular. They would never jump up and sit on the dasher if play got too close to them. On more than one occasion a little old lady with a hat pin would poke such a ref in the butt or smack him on the head with a newspaper (which hurts like hell for those who have never experienced such a smack), and as a result, it was good practice, and superstition, to avoid the dasher and have a good game.

In the television era, the referee who dropped the puck to start the game always had a superstition of signalling to the camera for his family watching at home. The ref knew that in those few moments before he dropped the puck the camera was fully focused on him while the play-by-play man announced the officiating crew. The ref would touch the collar of his sweater, flip the puck in the air, wink, or do something visual so that wife and kids would be able to know he was thinking of them. It was their good-luck charm, their final preparation to ensure that they had a good game.

SUPERSTITIONS ON AIR

Broadcasters can be superstitious as well, particularly when it comes to saying anything that might jinx the home team (or the team affiliated with the broadcaster). The most common example is a shutout for a goalie. If the home team is winning by a shutout early in the third period, the commentators will not refer to the goalie's shutout bid or anything associated with it (i.e., the number of shutouts the goalie has this season or in his career). Conversely, if the opposing goalie has a shutout going, the commentators won't hesitate to mention the fact, hoping to get their team a goal.

This superstition can carry weight for anything important—a big win, a record, an historic event of some sort.

FANDEMONIUM

Hockey would not be hockey without the fans, and who among its legions of followers is not superstitious? If the casual shinny player tries to emulate his idol by wearing a particular number, dressing a particular way, or skating like his hero, then fans are guilty of copycat superstitions to an even greater degree.

Where to start? Most any serious fan has a special chair or place to watch a game. If you sat on one end of a sofa when your team won, you must sit there for every game. Of course, who you watch the game with is also key. Some fans must watch with like-minded supporters, and some with the dreaded enemy for good luck. Watch a victory with one group of friends, and outsiders are not welcome to the next.

Watching a game must be done with clothing, often a key element in a team's victory. Wearing that raggedy-old shirt—or the team's official sweater—can make a huge difference, but so can slippers, hats, and any other paraphernalia kicking around the house.

Some fans must eat certain foods at certain times. Watch a game while eating pizza in the first period of a game that ends in victory and you must eat pizza every first period. The list is endless. Answer the phone during a game; never answer. Watch alone at home; watch in the same bar at the same stool. Shave before the opening faceoff; don't shave. Watch with the sound on or the volume button on mute. Listen to the radio play-by-play or watch the game on TV.

Sometimes the key to victory is predicting that the other team will win. The fan, of course, is never right, so better to say the bad guys will win because that guarantees the good guys will. Even better is for a fan to put his money where his mouth is.

Use a gambling platform to wager five dollars on his team's losing, and if he is right he'll double his money, and if wrong, even better—his team has won. And it cost only five bucks.

Unfortunately, sometimes the key to victory is *not* watching a game. It's frustrating, but on occasion very effective. Example: a fan's team is trailing 1–0. He goes to the bathroom, and when he comes back they've tied the game, 1–1. He decides to go away and do something else, and when he returns, the boys are winning, 3–1. At this point, the message is clear: stay away from the TV and his team will win.

Like players, fans also know that these things are best observed during the playoffs or for a crucial late-season game. Watching hockey is fun, so if fans spend the regular season not following these superstitions, that's okay, because even the top teams will lose twenty to thirty games a year. It's when a best-of-seven series is on the line and every game is critical that their superstitions must dictate and consume their lives fully.

PLAYER SUPERSTITIONS
To Each His (Crazy) Own

Overleaf: Goalie Gerry Cheevers marked his mask every time he got hit in the face with a puck.

KARL ALZNER: Crazy Eights

Drafted by the Washington Capitals in 2007, Karl Alzner is just beginning what could well be a long and successful career in the NHL. The defenceman has been playing on a team with Alexander Ovechkin, looks to be on a Stanley Cup contender for the foreseeable future, and will have a say as to whether the team can improve its fortunes even further by going all the way. He had an outstanding junior career with the Calgary Hitmen in the Western Hockey League, and he won two gold medals with Canada at the World Junior Championship (in 2007 and 2008). He also played for Canada at the 2007 Super Series, an eight-game showdown dominated by Canada against the Russians (seven wins and a tie in eight games).

Alzner has been trying to rid himself of a couple loopy superstitions. These take place during the playing of "O Canada" before the opening faceoff. While listening to the song, Alzner taps his stick eighty-eight times and makes an outline of the Canadian flag on the ice. He has come to realize these actions drive him crazy, however, and more recently has adopted a simpler superstition. He wears two bracelets—blue and brown—made for him by his girlfriend. As he sees it, they stay on his wrist until they break.

SERGE AUBRY: *Sartorial Exorcism*

There has always been a clear hierarchy in hockey. The NHL is the pinnacle, the best league to which all pros aspire. Below that is a succession of lower leagues, each clearly a step below the previous. In the early 1970s, with the World Hockey Association in the mix, that hierarchy was even richer. In order, the list looks something like this: NHL, WHA, AHL (American Hockey League), IHL (International Hockey League), and CHL (Central Hockey League). Below the CHL are other even smaller leagues from which no player ever emerged to play in the NHL.

Goalie Serge Aubry, though, made an impressive rise for several seasons. The Montreal native turned pro with the Tulsa Oilers in 1967, the year the NHL expanded from six teams to twelve. The Oilers were a CHL team, and over the course of the next three years Aubry enjoyed success with them. He eventually moved up to the AHL and then signed with the Quebec Nordiques in 1972 when the WHA began. Aubry played there for five years but was never able to get to the NHL.

Clearly, though, the roots of his success were with the Oilers, and he attributed part of that success to a lucky blue suit that he wore all the time.

There came a day, however, when the suit no longer favoured him with the glory he had come to expect of it, so he enlisted the help of some teammates to rid the world of this once-fine garment.

He took the suit to a friend's lawn, where several players stomped on it, spat on it, and more or less treated it with the lack of respect that it had come to deserve. Aubry then doused the suit with gas, added a match to the deal, and burned the suit into oblivion. The hockey world had one less superstition to concern itself with.

ED BELFOUR: Noli Me Equipment Tangere

Have you ever seen a screaming eagle? There was one sure way to witness the scary spectacle if you happened to play on the same team as goaltender Ed Belfour, nicknamed "Eddie the Eagle."

Despite being ignored in the Entry Draft, Belfour went on to become one of the winningest goalies in NHL history. He always wore number 20 when it was available, to honour his childhood hero, Vladislav Tretiak, and he always had an eagle painted on the side of his mask (to honour the nickname).

Proving there is more to the man than meets the eye, Belfour is also an avid collector of fine cars and owns his own auto restoration business. He also holds a pilot's licence.

Belfour retired in the summer of 2009 after seventeen NHL seasons and one final year playing in Sweden. Wherever he played he was consistent in one regard—no one was allowed to touch his equipment. No one means *no one*. It was a superstition that will help get him into the Hockey Hall of Fame one day, that's for sure.

BILL BEVERIDGE: *Hey, Buddy*

A goalie from 1929 to 1943, Bill Beveridge is the perfect example of just how tough it was to play in the NHL in the decades before expansion. Despite being a superb goalie, he spent most of his fourteen seasons in the minors or at the end of the bench in the NHL.

His first season of pro hockey came with the Detroit Cougars in the days before the team was known as the Red Wings, but it didn't go well, and he was a part-timer with Ottawa the next year and in the minors the year after. He later played with two teams that became defunct—the St. Louis Eagles and the Montreal Maroons—and finished with the New York Rangers. In between, he spent most of his time in the IAHL (International–American Hockey League) and then later in the renamed AHL.

Beveridge liked to choose a teammate to sit beside in the dressing room. He'd have that player as a stall friend until the team lost, after which he'd settle in beside someone else. In 1938–39, he went even one superstition further. He partnered with Bob McCully for most of the year, but Beveridge could not leave the dressing room until he said, "Move over, Bob" at least once.

PETER BONDRA: *Counting One to Five*

Superstitions rise to this status by virtue of their success. No one maintains superstitions that lead to demotions, failed careers, and lousy results. Those are the habits that are quickly replaced.

Peter Bondra, whose outstanding goal-scoring abilities took a back seat to those of precious few players during his career, had a superstition that became a vital part of his success. And, like most goal scorers, the superstition had to do with his sticks.

Bondra retired in 2007 having had an impact in both the NHL and the international game, for his native Slovakia. In the case of the former, he scored

503 career goals and twice led the league in this statistic (thirty-four in 1994–95 and fifty-two in 1997–98) before the introduction of the Rocket Richard Trophy. Bondra played the vast majority of his seventeen pro seasons with the Washington Capitals and settled near D.C. after his playing days were over. This despite having scored the most important goal in Slovakian history.

That came in 2002 at the World Championship when he had the game winner with 1:40 left in the third period of the gold-medal game against Russia. The historic victory was the new country's first gold since declaring independence from the Czechs in 1993 and was, for his country, of the same magnitude as Paul Henderson's goal for Canada at the 1972 Summit Series.

Bondra's superstition was straightforward. For the pre-game skate he would use five sticks. Numbering them, he would decide which one felt like his "game stick" and begin the first period with it. If he scored, he'd keep using it. If he grew restless, he'd put it aside and try another number. Ironically, one of Bondra's greatest accomplishments came the night of February 5, 1994, when he scored five goals in a single game. No word on what number stick he used, but all five likely came using the same twig.

QUICKSHOT DANIEL BOUCHARD

A long-time goalie with the Atlanta Flames in the 1970s, and the idol of a teenaged Patrick Roy, Daniel Bouchard had one superstition that was, if nothing else, unique. At the end of every period, he'd skate as hard as he could to the players' bench, wanting to work up a bit of a sweat at the end of the period.

BRUCE BOUDREAU: *Groundhog Day*

It's difficult to imagine that Washington Capitals coach Bruce Boudreau can have any superstitions worthy of his time or effort. After all, it took him seventeen years in the minors as a coach to reach the NHL after a playing career similarly mired by the minor leagues. That is, Boudreau spent seventeen years on skates during which time he appeared in just 141 NHL games, mostly with Toronto. He was deemed too small for the ever-growing league and was called up time and again for brief stints as a fill-in for various injured players.

Despite a lack of NHL success, Boudreau had a tremendous career in the AHL, IHL, and CHL, however, and always found a team to play for. When he retired in 1992, he turned to coaching and was just as successful—in the minors, of course. As a player might, he worked his way up through the chain of leagues that connect, eventually, to the NHL. He started in the IHL with Fort Wayne, down to Mississippi of the East Coast Hockey League (ECHL), and then established himself in the AHL with Lowell. Boudreau remained in the AHL for the better part of nine years before being called up to coach the Capitals after the team fired Glen Hanlon in 2007. There has been no looking back since, and Boudreau does his superstitious part to make sure he remains in the top league.

When he gets to the arena, he'll eat the meal provided in the media room if it brings him good luck. If he has eaten the meal at that particular arena previously and lost the game, no meal for him. When the team is winning, he'll keep wearing the same suit. If he talks to someone on the phone before what turns out to be a win, he'll call that person before every game until the team loses.

In one instance, he asked Viktor Kozlov how he was doing before a game. The team won, so Boudreau made a point of asking Kozlov how he was before the next several games, resulting in a winning streak. When you make it to the NHL full-time at age fifty-three, you'll do whatever you can to stay there.

RAY BOURQUE: Lace 'Em Up, Over and Over

Although Ray Bourque couldn't bring the Stanley Cup to Boston as a leader, he ended up with his name on the cherished trophy after hitching a ride with a team destined for victory. The Colorado Avalanche won the Cup in 2000–01, and Bourque retired that summer, the final piece of his Hall of Fame career in place.

He sweated profusely during games, which is why he always used several pairs of gloves over the course of an evening. After coming off the ice he'd hand his gloves to a trainer, who would in turn hand him a dry pair. This, of course, isn't superstition so much as equipment management, but Bourque also liked to change his skate laces during every intermission. At the end of the game, he'd throw them all out. Now *this* is the stuff of superstition.

As well, Bourque got into the habit of saying good luck to the goalie before the opening faceoff. It all began with a goalie named Marco Baron in the early 1980s. Baron never became a full-time goalie with the Bruins, but before one game Bourque tapped him on the blocker, then the outside of the left pad and the right pad, then a short smack to, yes, the jock. The team won the game, and this little sequence became Bourque's signature for the rest of his career. As the "Star-Spangled Banner" neared its conclusion, Bourque bent down quickly to touch the ice with his right hand, blessed himself, and then skated off like the wind, ready to play.

JOHNNY BOWER: Ancient Beliefs

The oldest goalie in NHL history, Johnny Bower had a sensational AHL career in the minors before embarking on a lengthy career with the Leafs during their period of greatest glory, the 1960s. He was nicknamed the "China Wall" for his longevity, and, of course, his bravery in playing the position bare-faced becomes only more legendary with the passing of every day.

But Bower had several superstitions to help calm his nerves and ensure victory—or at least allowed him to play well. For starters, he'd always save a stick he used in a shutout, making sure he didn't practise with it and wear it out. He had to be the first player out of the dressing room for every game or practice, and he dressed left to right.

As he stood in the crease listening to the national anthem, Bower contemplated the action he would have to deal with for the next two hours, but as soon as "O Canada" had finished, he tapped his right pad with his stick and was ready to go.

When the team travelled, by plane or bus, Bower had to sit in the front seat next to the door, and beside him teammate Marcel Pronovost had to sit. In that way did the "China Wall" win the Stanley Cup four times in six years, including 1967, the last time the Leafs won the sacred bowl.

DARREN BOYKO: *Time to Worry*

Although he is one of a short list of players to have appeared in a single NHL game, Darren Boyko had a lengthy career in Europe, principally Finland, where he was later inducted into its national hockey hall of fame.

A two-way skater, faceoff artiste, top scorer, and team player, Boyko had one particularly odd superstition that worked in direct contrast to 1960s Leafs coach Punch Imlach's. Boyko never looked at a clock when it read 11:11. "If I saw that time, the team or I would have a bad game," he confessed. How he came to associate bad luck with the time 11:11 is a mystery even to him, but it stuck with him for a decade and more until he came home, retired, and never worried about time again. Imlach, on the other hand, revered the number for its good fortune.

DANIEL BRIÈRE: Do Unto Other Sticks As You Would Have Them Do Unto You

When he signed an eight-year, $52 million contract with the Philadelphia Flyers in 2007, Daniel Brière established himself as one of the top-paid players in the NHL. He earned the deal as a result of his ability to score thirty goals a season (not to mention his status as an unrestricted free agent), but injuries have played a part in a lack of consistency since then.

Brière has won a gold medal for Canada at the U18 Championship (1994), World Junior Championship (1997), and World Championship (2003 and 2004). Having a good relationship with his sticks is essential to his success, and Brière has two particular superstitions in this regard.

First, he likes to talk to his sticks before a game, just to make sure they know what they're supposed to do and what he expects of them. Second, he always prepares three sticks for every game. Whenever he plays well with one, though, he doesn't keep using it, as would most players. Instead, he gives it a game off or a day off to allow it to rest, just as a coach might a player or a team after an excellent game.

Other players would work the stick like a horse, whipping every ounce of strength out of it before

throwing it away. But not Brière. More compassionate, he'd prefer to extend the life of the stick by using
it judiciously and with paternal care instead.

MARTIN BRODEUR: Family and Hockey Can Coexist

By the time he retires, Martin Brodeur will hold every
major record for goalies in NHL history. He will have
played more games and minutes, won more games,
and recorded more shutouts than anyone else since
the NHL first began in 1917. So whatever he does to
prepare himself for a game must work.

In his case, it's family that matters most. He
comes from a big family of two brothers and two
sisters. The patriarch, Denis Sr., played goal for
Canada at the 1956 Olympics, winning a bronze
medal, and he later became the photographer for
the Canadiens for decades. Denis Jr. has followed
in his father's footsteps to become a photographer,
while Claude was a Montreal Expos prospect at
one time. Denis Sr. and Martin are the only father-
son tandem in Canadian history to have both won
Olympic medals in hockey, Martin doing his part
by leading Canada to gold in 2002 in Salt Lake City.

Martin also has four children from his first wife,
Melanie: Anthony, William and Jeremy (twins), and

Annabelle. He has their initials on the back of his mask. He also uses a new stick for every game he plays, and before every game he writes their names on its shaft, believing they will bring him luck. Those sticks have done wonders for Martin.

PETER BUDAJ: D'oh

One of more than 150 players to graduate from the legendary St. Michael's high school in Toronto to go on to the NHL, Peter Budaj has had a tough time establishing himself as a number-one goalie. He was drafted by the Colorado Avalanche in 2001 and was given every opportunity to be the heir to Patrick Roy's crease, but Budaj has struggled to deliver what Avs management was hoping for. However, he is still a world-class goalie for Slovakia and has played in both the 2004 World Cup and 2006 Olympics for his country.

The most outlandish feature of Budaj's appearance is his masks, which have had several cartoon characters adorning them, including many from The Simpsons and video games.

Budaj is a creature of habit on game days, and his exact routine is an important part of his mental and physical preparation. He will wake up at 7:30

a.m., have a bowl of cereal and coffee, and get to the rink by 8:30 a.m. He goes through an extensive warm-up for the morning skate, after which he has his main meal of the day.

In Budaj's case, that means salmon with either pasta or rice. His preference is to stop by the same restaurant and take the meal home with him. After that, he must have a long nap, then get to the arena two hours before the game to do the same prep as he did in the morning before the light skate. Practise makes perfect.

GERRY CHEEVERS: *Better the Mask than the Face*

To this day, the masks of Gerry Cheevers are arguably the best the game has ever seen. Cheevers played for Boston at a time when goalies were making the transition from playing without a mask to playing with one. When Cheevers played junior with St. Mike's in Toronto, he was bare-faced, but by the time he got to the Bruins he was wearing facial protection.

The late 1960s and early 1970s was a period of controversy and discomfort for goalies. It was an awkward and lengthy transition, not a simple case of no mask one day and mask the next day. Goalies

Goalie Gerry Cheevers marked his mask every time he got hit in the face by a puck.

were vilified for wearing them, called cowards
by their own coaches and managers. Masks were
crudely and inconsistently crafted, and many were
uncomfortable or prevented a goalie from seeing
the puck at his skates.

Different styles and designs of masks had different advantages but also different problems, and
all didn't protect the face completely. Eyes were still
vulnerable, and the mask was still right up against
a goalie's skin, meaning if a hard slapshot hit it, the
goalie would still be cut and seriously injured.

Cheevers painted black scars on his mask every time he was hit by a puck. It was a symbol for all to see that without the mask, this is where he'd have required stitches. It was his superstition that so long as he painted the scars on the mask, he himself wouldn't be seriously hurt.

The masks gave him an eerie and menacing look as well, but it worked more as a reminder that a mask was effective for preventing many an injury, something no coach or manager could rightly complain about. And for Cheevers, the mask gave him confidence to play aggressively and not worry about being hurt, the most difficult task any goalie of his era faced.

QUICK SHOT CHRIS CHELIOS

Chris Chelios always had to be the last player to be fully dressed before going out on the ice. The twenty-five-year NHL veteran was the second-oldest skater in NHL history by the time he played his last game in 2010.

JACQUES CLOUTIER: *Red Is the Colour of Victory*

While most goalies don't particularly like the colour red because it connotes the goal lamp, Jacques Cloutier was just the opposite. During a career with Buffalo, Chicago, and Quebec between 1981 and 1994, he always wore a red tie before an important game. If he lost a game after wearing that tie, his wife would have to go out and buy another red tie. "He must have had 50 or 60 ties in his wardrobe," quipped Buffalo teammate Mike Foligno.

SIDNEY CROSBY: *Sorry, Mom, Can't Talk*

You would think he's so good just because he's so good, but think about the superstitions of Wayne Gretzky. Then multiply by a thousand or so and you get the level of superstition Sidney Crosby brings to the rink every day. Indeed, as he will say to defend his privacy, he's so superstitious that one of his superstitions is not to talk about them!

Still, word gets out and teammates leak bits of information on the subject, and Crosby himself will 'fess up to a thing or two. For starters, he must walk through the Mellon Arena from the street outside to the dressing room taking the same path, going through certain doors, past certain fixed objects. It is a route created by Crosby himself and it makes no sense to the common walker.

At the entrance to the dressing room he takes off his street shoes. These never touch the sanctity of the room, so if he walks out having forgotten something, he'll take his shoes off before returning to get the item.

Even stranger is his eating habits. He's not particular about what kinds of food he eats, but when he sits down he must have Maxime Talbot on his left and Pascal Dupuis on his right. Anyone who alters this order is not well versed in Crosby-ania.

Crosby's main concern is his sticks. Once he's taped them and put them in position for the game, no one can touch them. The tape is like a safe, and once it's on the sticks they belong to him and only him. If someone does touch one, he'll take the tape off and redo it.

Pity his mother. Crosby also refuses to talk to her on game day because every time he has done so in the past he has been injured.

As for the team, his role as captain allows him some power for success. That is, he likes to stay at the same hotel so long as the team is winning, but a loss means the end to that hotel. This was most conspicuous during the 2009 Cup finals against

Detroit. When the Penguins travelled to Michigan for games, they stayed at a different hotel than in 2008, when the Red Wings won the Cup at Pittsburgh's expense.

And one last one for the road, as it were. Whenever the team bus goes over a railway crossing, Crosby raises his legs and touches the window. Go figure.

WILF CUDE: Rabbit's Foot—or Not

Plenty of players have superstitions that take the form of a good-luck charm, something tangible they keep in their stall or travel with, but surely goalie Wilf Cude was the one and only player who brought his charm out onto the ice with him.

A goalie in the 1930s, Cude played for five teams, most impressively with the Montreal Canadiens, with whom he played nearly every minute of every game from 1928 to 1938. His best year came about by accident. He started 1933–34 with the Canadiens but after one game was loaned to Detroit for a year. Cude took the team to the Stanley Cup finals before losing to Chicago.

Cude always played with a rabbit's foot in the top of one of his pads. Before every game he stuffed it in, and after every game he took it out. One day, a mouse got at it in the dressing room, and Cude never found it or replaced it. He continued to play with the same pads, but his rabbit's-footless luck managed to hold up for the rest of his career (although he never did win the Cup).

QUICK SHOT JOE DALEY

Goalie Joe Daley got his big break with expansion in 1967, first in the NHL and later for the Winnipeg Jets of the WHA, for whom he played the entire seven years of the league's existence. Daley always started getting dressed exactly half an hour before the pre-game skate, putting on only his socks, pads, and pants. With fifteen minutes to go, he put on the rest of his equipment.

GERRY DESJARDINS: Personal GPS at Work

Buffalo Sabres goalie Gerry Desjardins played parts of four seasons in Buffalo at the end of his career. He had played previously with Los Angeles, Chicago, and the New York Islanders, but he played more games with Buffalo than any other team. His superstition was straightforward. He always drove from his home to the Buffalo Memorial Auditorium along the same route.

Desjardins believed it only made sense to be as uniform in this aspect of game-day preparations as in the dressing room, during warm-up, or during stoppages of play. The trouble was that his personal GPS took him through streets that were sometimes a nightmare to navigate during the many and severe winter storms Buffalo is subject to, but that made little difference to the diminutive goalie. Every game, same roads.

Still, he was aware of the folly and brittle nature of superstitions. He liked to have a coffee before every game, but one time he decided not to and he still played well. The coffee superstition was no more.

SHANE DOAN: *Good Player, Good Book*

One of the most respected players in the game, Shane Doan has experienced the highs and lows of being an NHLer. In a game on December 13, 2005, he was accused of making a racial slur against a French-Canadian official, a charge that was never founded or punished. Doan has represented his country internationally on several occasions,

Shane Doan gets a little luck and inspiration from a Biblical reference he writes on all his sticks.

including at six World Championships and the 2004 World Cup of Hockey. He has been captain on several occasions and is known to be a God-fearing man incapable of swearing or taking the Lord's name in vain.

Doan has played his entire career with Winnipeg/Phoenix. His rookie season, 1995–96, was the last for the Jets in Manitoba, and the next year the team transferred to Arizona and he with it. He became Coyotes captain in 2003, a position he has held ever since.

For Doan, the very concept of superstition is superseded by his religious beliefs, but that doesn't mean the two can't go together. That is, it's one thing for a player to believe in God, but it's another to ask God, as it were, for a little extra help at the arena.

In Doan's case, it is a short passage from the Book of Jeremiah, chapter 29, verse 11. The passage reads: "For I know the plans I have for you, plans to prosper you and not to harm you, plans to give you hope and a future." For this reason, Doan has always written "29:11" on all his sticks since 1995.

KEN DRYDEN: Smart, but Superstitious All the Same

Despite being one of the more learned specimens of hockey player, goalie Ken Dryden was not above being lured into the murky underworld of super-stitious folly like his puck-playing colleagues. In his case, they numbered several, all of them as erudite or ridiculous as anyone else's.

Most of Dryden's superstitions had to do with his time on ice before a game. For starters, he had to fire the first puck of the pre-game skate wide and to the right, hitting the boards. If he hit the glass or failed to raise the puck at all, he would play poorly. But if he hit the boards themselves, he'd play well.

At the end of the warm-up, he always had to make one final save before skating off. Never leave the ice after allowing a goal on the last shot, he believed. Teammate Larry Robinson figured this out and made sure to snap an easy one for Dryden to pick off, but Dryden figured out his teammate's generosity and made the last pre-Robinson save the important one.

One day Dryden said a few words to an usherette named Joyce who worked behind the visitors' bench. He played well that night and then made it a point to look at her during the warm-up every home game. After he lost a game, he never looked at Joyce again. Poor dear.

Most commonsensical was the final moment before the opening faceoff. With the players lined up at centre ice, the referee performed one last duty before dropping the puck. He'd look to one end, where the goal judge would flash the red goal light to indicate it was working; then he'd do the same at the other end. Dryden made a point of not looking at the red light when it flashed on. The last thing he needed right before the opening faceoff was a reminder of being scored upon.

PHIL ESPOSITO: *Lord, There Goes a Scorer*

"Espo" may or may not have been raised a good Catholic, but he has a connection to the church nonetheless. By the time Phil Esposito retired, only Gordie Howe had scored more often, but Esposito's forte was a quick shot from the slot. This gave rise to a famous fan placard that appeared at the Boston Garden: "Jesus Saves . . . but Espo scores on the rebound."

Phil Esposito was famous for the black turtleneck he wore throughout his NHL career.

Indeed, Esposito had the five greatest seasons in hockey history (all in a row) between 1970–71 and 1974–75 when he had at least 55 goals and 127 points in each season. In the first of that run, he set records for goals (76) and points (152) in one year, records that endured until Wayne Gretzky came into the league almost a decade later.

Esposito started his career with the Chicago Black Hawks, but a huge deal that also brought Ken Hodge and Fred Stanfield to the Bruins proved a turning point in league history. The Hawks made one of the worst deals of all time; the Bruins one of the best. Esposito arrived by saying the team would make the playoffs in his first year, win a round the year after, and win the Stanley Cup in his third year. Guess what? He was right.

To be sure, he was a superstitious player as well. This is evident from any photograph of him in a Boston sweater. He always wore a black turtleneck underneath his equipment—backward. Like so many other tales, this was the result of found luck. He was suffering from a cold before one game, put on a turtleneck for extra warmth, and played well. The turtleneck stayed with him the rest of his career, and, thankfully, he was pragmatic enough not to worry about it going unwashed. He maintained his superstition *and* he smelled good, too.

"Espo" also liked to drive to the Boston Garden using the same route, and during the national anthem he always said a prayer asking for a good game and to make sure no player on either side suffered a serious injury. He hated crossed sticks as well, guaranteeing bad luck whenever he saw them. "I don't like to see crossed sticks in the dressing room. It's a bad omen. It means somebody is going to get hurt on the ice. Not just for your team; maybe on the other. I've seen it happen numerous times."

Esposito always kept good-luck charms from fans in his stall with Italian peppers, and always had a stick of gum at his side while he dressed. On road trips, he never stayed on the thirteenth floor or in a room that ended in the number 13.

Whether they're superstitions or religious beliefs, they all amount to the same thing. Do what feels comfortable, and performance will take care of itself. With some 717 regular-season goals, "Espo" was a believer.

TONY ESPOSITO: *Just Let Them Be*

One of the greatest brother combinations in hockey history was the forward–goalie tandem of Phil and Tony Esposito of Sault Ste. Marie, Ontario. While

Phil forged a Hall of Fame career as a scorer, his brother was going the same way from the crease as a preventer of goals, a task he performed masterfully for nearly two decades.

While Phil was nicknamed "Espo," his brother was called "Tony O," the "O" representing both the last letter of his last name and also a shutout, appropriate for a goalie who retired with seventy-six shutouts, including a modern-day record of fifteen in one season, 1969–70. For eight straight seasons (1973–81), he played at least sixty-three games, including back-to-back seasons of seventy and seventy-one games in 1973–74 and 1974–75. These came in a seventy-six-game season, proof of his durability and exceptional play.

Just as Jesse James would have been particularly fussy about his guns, so, too, was "Tony O" particularly particular about his sticks. He positioned them in the stick rack and by his dressing room stall in a specific way, and he hated having this setup tampered with. Crossed sticks sent him off the deep end, and any appearance that deviated from what he desired was destined to be bad luck. With 423 wins under his Hall of Fame belt, this was not a lot to ask for.

QUICKSHOT BOB ESSENSA

Goalie Bob Essensa wasn't finicky about the stick he used in games, but he was very finicky about his second stick, the one a goalie always keeps at the bench in case his game stick breaks. Essensa—this is the truth!—never used his second stick! If his game stick broke, the trainer had to go to the dressing room to get a new stick, not the one from the stick rack by the players' bench.

RAY FERRARO: Chicken Parm for All Times

Superstitions invariably start because of some immediate success associated with a particular activity accidentally or unknowingly performed, but they end for a variety of reasons. Of course, any superstition shouldn't end until it has ceased to be effective, but in the case of Ray Ferraro it may have been sheer boredom that ended one of his rituals.

Over a career that spanned 18 seasons and 1,258 games, Ferraro scored an impressive 408 goals, although he never won the Stanley Cup (coming closest in 1993 with the New York Islanders when the team advanced as far as the semi-finals).

Ferraro's pre-game meal one time consisted of chicken parmesan. He went out and scored two goals. For two years he ate nothing but chicken parmesan before games, and no one is certain whether a scoring drought or sheer fatigue of this good but hardly exceptional meal caused him to stop.

In 2002, he retired and became a television commentator, starting with ESPN. He later became known as "chicken parm" because one night just before air time he ate the meal again and spilled some on his shirt and tie. With no time to change, he had to cover the bad stains repeatedly while he worked on air, much to the delight of his colleagues.

QUICKSHOT BOB GAINEY

He was called the most complete player in the world by legendary Soviet coach Viktor Tikhonov. Bob Gainey, the long-time captain of the Montreal Canadiens, reportedly confessed this about his main superstition: "In between periods, I always ask for a drink made with 30 per cent Coke and 50 per cent water. I've had this habit ever since I started to play for the Canadiens." Be that as it may, his glass was still 20 per cent empty.

QUICK SHOT BERT GARDINER

Bert Gardiner managed to tend the goal of four Original Six teams in the 1930s and 1940s—New York, Montreal, Chicago, and Boston—and he is proof that superstitions either get handed down from one generation to the next or that players from different eras are more similar than one might think. Today, we know Sidney Crosby enters the Mellon Arena through the same door and has a series of routines to get him into the dressing room. Well, in this same vein, Gardiner always entered the arena he was playing in through the same door, and he also took the same path to get to the dressing room, no matter how tangled or non-linear that route might be.

BRUCE GARDINER: Potty Trained

Bruce Gardiner skated in 312 regular-season games, not an enormous number, but 312 more than most people in the world. The highlight of his career was the four seasons he played in Ottawa (1996–2000). Alas, trivia buffs might rather focus on his time with the Columbus Blue Jackets because Gardiner scored the first goal in that franchise's history.

But back to Ottawa. Gardiner was drafted by St. Louis in 1991, but it wasn't until five years later that he finally made the NHL, with the Senators. In between, he had finished his career and degree at Colgate University and played two years in the AHL with Ottawa's affiliate in Prince Edward Island. Never a great scorer, he was nevertheless not strictly a checking forward; he needed to make at least some contribution to the offence if he were going to stick with the team. However, he got off to a slow start and worried about his scoring.

This is where teammate Tom Chorske stepped in. Chorske suggested that Gardiner was treating his stick with too much respect, and to teach it a lesson he should dunk it in the toilet before going out on the ice. Gardiner dutifully took the advice and plunked the blade of his stick into the toilet water, went out, and played a great game.

And so was born one of the nuttiest superstitions of all time. Before every game, Gardiner would wet his stick in the toilet to help him play better. It gave him 312 games, plus dozens more in Russia, Finland, and the minors, so it did him more good than harm.

BOYD GORDON (AND MATT BRADLEY):
A Most Delicate Touch

There is weird and then there is *weird,* and you can file this under *weird.*

Boyd Gordon and Matt Bradley are two important pieces to the emerging Stanley Cup puzzle that is the Washington Capitals. Although the team is led by Alexander Ovechkin, with a strong supporting cast that includes defenceman Mike Green and youngsters Nicklas Backstrom and Alexander Semin, Gordon and Bradley are important elements on a team that will be challenging for the Stanley Cup for years to come.

Bradley was drafted by San Jose back in 1996 but has been with the Caps for five seasons. The right winger is known more for his defensive work than his touch around the net, although he did manage two goals in fourteen games in the 2008 playoffs.

Gordon is a half a generation younger, having been selected seventeenth overall by the Caps in 2002. He has played all his NHL games with Washington, and he played for Canada against Ovechkin in the gold-medal game of the 2003 World Junior Championship.

Nothing can reasonably explain how and why this superstition came to be, but teammate Brooks

Laich explains it as delicately as anyone, albeit between laughs: "Before every game Brads has to go over to Gordo and tap him in the jock." Laugh. Pause. "It's so funny," Laich continues, "because neither can play unless he does it!"

And so the definition of superstition falls below the belt, as it were.

SCOTT GORDON: *Get a Grip*

Although Scott Gordon got his first NHL head coaching job with the New York Islanders on August 12, 2008, his connection to hockey goes way back. As a goalie, he was the first player to go from the ECHL to the NHL, in 1989, with the Quebec Nordiques. He played just twenty-one NHL games, all with the Nords, but he enjoyed a fine career in the minors and was also a member of Team USA for the 1992 Olympics.

As a goalie, he was superstitious about dressing before the game to such an extent that he actually had to stop because he was driving himself crazy. "I was pretty particular about getting dressed by segments of time," he admitted.

These segments were a slow and deliberate process intended to get him into a rhythm that would continue through sixty minutes of hockey. Exactly half an hour before the game he'd put on some of his equipment; ten minutes later, more equipment. Ten minutes to game time, the final pieces.

Fortunately, he discarded the code by the time he made it to the Nordiques. As he admitted, the superstition "started to rule my life as far as second-guessing myself. Did I remember to do this? Did I remember to do that? By the time I turned pro, I learned that there were too many games to maintain all of those superstitions."

After retiring in 1994, Gordon immediately went into coaching, starting in the IHL, where, at age thirty, he was among the youngest coaches in league history. He moved to Providence of the AHL, going from assistant coach to head coach, and for several years kept the Bruins among the league's elite teams.

"RED" GOUPILLE: The Real Thing

Cliff "Red" Goupille, who played 222 NHL games with the Canadiens in the 1930s and 1940s, had a strange superstition. He liked to put a bottle of Coke in one of his shoes, guaranteeing he'd score when he did. This either wasn't the real reason or it was the worst superstition of all time.

Goupille was a defenceman at a time when that position required only meticulous play in his own end. Offence, if not altogether forbidden, was surely not encouraged by coaches. "Red" scored but twelve career goals in the NHL, never more than three in any one season between 1935 and 1943. His minor-league career was no more prodigious—he scored six times in the Quebec senior league with Sherbrooke in 1948–49. That's a lot of Coke for a little return.

QUICKSHOT RON GRAHAME

Goalie Ron Grahame is part of two distinctive pieces of trivia. He is one of a rare group of father–son goalie tandems in NHL history; his son, John, playing in the twenty-first century after Grahame played in the late 1970s. However, the only member of the Grahame family whose name appears on the Stanley Cup is Charlotte Grahame, Ron's wife and John's mother. She was a member of the Colorado Avalanche front office when the Avs won the Cup in 2001. Ron's superstition varied only slightly over the course of his career. He stood either in his crease or at the blue line for the national anthem, changing his position based on having won or lost the previous game.

"CAMMI" GRANATO: What a Doll

During her fifteen-year career with the U.S. national team, Catherine "Cammi" Granato set every scoring record for her country and was among the top scorers of all-time in modern women's hockey.

She played at nine World Women's Championships as well as the first two Olympics with women's participation (1998 and 2002), winning one gold in each and silver in every other year (beating, or being beaten by, Canada in each case).

Granato was a pure scorer, and her final statistics tell as much: fifty-four games played in these tournaments, fifty-four goals, and ninety-six total points. She was among the first group of three women inducted into the International Ice Hockey Federation (IIHF) Hall of Fame in 2008 (along with Canadians Geraldine Heaney and Angela James). Her career had ended surprisingly, when Team USA coach Ben Smith cut her from the team just before the start of the 2006 Olympics in Turin (during which, and not surprisingly, the Americans had their worst showing, managing only a bronze medal).

Throughout her years the one constant in her life was her good-luck beanbag frog called "Floppy." It went everywhere with her. Furthermore, on ice, she liked to tap one post, then the other, and finally the crossbar for good luck. Such modest superstitions, but such lofty results.

"WIN" GREEN: Trained to Win (or Tie)

A long-time trainer for the Boston Bruins, "Win" Green came from the black-and-white era of hockey's early days before the Original Six got its name and before the NHL was limited to only six teams. That is, he was around in the 1930s when the Bruins were developing into a consistently good team with the Kraut Line of Milt Schmidt–Bobby Bauer–Woody Dumart.

In these days, the team played at the old Boston Garden, and the arena was unique in hockey because it connected directly to the train station, the North Station downtown. Players, officials, and staff almost all took the subway from their homes or hotels because they could get off a train, walk along a short tunnel, and enter the Garden directly.

It was along this journey, though, that the pedestrian encountered three turnstiles. In Green's estimation, the one on the left meant win, the middle one meant tie, and the right one represented loss. Of course, Green was honest in his assessment of how the team was playing and who the opponent was that night, so sometimes he entered the "win" turnstile and sometimes the "tie." But he never, ever used the "lose" turnstile!

WAYNE GRETZKY: Not Too Good for the Rest of Us

Anyone who dismisses superstitions better not say so near the "Great One," Wayne Gretzky. By the time he retired, he held more than sixty NHL records and to this day remains—by a huge margin—the all-time leader in goals, assists, and total points. Yet for all his spontaneous genius during games, he went through a carefully calculated series of rituals at the pre-game skate and in the dressing room before the opening faceoff.

Let's start in the dressing room. Gretzky always put on his equipment in the same order and always left to right: left shin pad, then stocking, right shin pad, stocking. After putting on his pants, he slid into his left skate, then right skate. Shoulder pads came next, then elbow pads, again left before right. He then put on his sweater and tucked the right side in at the back, perhaps his best-known identifier.

Out on the ice for the warm-up, Gretzky always fired the first puck wide and to the right of the goal, a rather humorous habit of intentional misfiring given that he scored more goals than anyone in the game's history.

Once the skate was over and the Zamboni circled the ice for a final flood before the start of a game, Gretzky headed back to the dressing room for a series of four beverages, in a particular order: Diet Coke, ice water, Gatorade, and a second Diet Coke.

Wayne Gretzky didn't play for St. Louis for very long but his habit of tucking in the back right side of his sweater was one that endured for all his 20 NHL seasons.

Perhaps his oddest superstition was his refusal to get his hair cut during road trips. "The last time I did," he once recounted, "we lost." That's how these things begin.

GLENN HALL: *The Fine Art of Upchucking*

In Original Six hockey, there were no off-nights. Sure, some teams were better than others, but when only six teams held the best players in the world, every night produced great hockey. This meant there were no easy nights for the goalies, no easy wins, no light games, especially since they played every minute without a mask.

Glenn Hall was a great among even the greatest, the goalie who played every minute for 502 consecutive games, a record that will never be bettered. Never. Guaranteed.

What is more amazing about Hall and his bare-faced brethren of six-team hockey was that they were so good for so long despite hating the game. They routinely suffered facial cuts or worse. Fans booed every goal they allowed. The pressure to succeed was enormous. Roger Crozier retired because of nerves. Terry Sawchuk left the game for the same reason mid-career. Gump Worsley hated flying and left. Hall hated training camp and practice because he'd suffer injuries for no good reason, as he saw it.

Hall was called "Mr. Goalie" as a parallel compliment to Gordie Howe's "Mr. Hockey" moniker, but Hall's habit—it can't rightly be called a superstition—was one for the ages. He threw up before every game he played. Nerves got the better of him. Motivating himself made him sick. Pressure weighed heavily on his insides. Every game he played started with a trip to the washroom. He was one of the greatest, but you certainly don't get the sense he enjoyed every minute of it.

DOUG HARVEY: *Always a Close Shave*

In the modern hockey world, players are covered in equipment from head to toe, so even in close-up only the front of their visage can be seen by fans watching on TV. But in the old days, when helmets were not part of the game, a player's appearance was part of his on-ice personality. Think of the long curly locks of Ron Duguay or "the blond demon" Guy Lafleur streaking up ice; the headband worn by Henry Boucha; the meticulous coif of Bobby Orr.

In the Original Six, facial hair was non-existent, as owners expected their players to be well groomed

Montreal's Doug Harvey shaved before every game for good luck.

on and off the ice. In the 1970s, wild haircuts became more common as players began to express themselves more freely in the era of the Players' Association and increased rights.

For Doug Harvey, one of the greatest defencemen of all time, his regimen was simple. He shaved before every game. This was part superstition, part practical. On the one hand, a clean-shaven face felt good for him and made him play better. On the other hand, as goalie Turk Broda used to say, a clean face stitches easier. And, truth be told, not a game went by without at least a couple of players requiring stitches, so it was always better to make that part of the evening as painless and seamless as possible.

Looks were important for Harvey, but with or without the smooth face, he always looked good when he played.

QUICK SHOT JOHAN HEDBERG

When goalie Johan Hedberg made his NHL debut, with Pittsburgh in 2000–01, it was as a last-minute call-up from the AHL's Manitoba Moose. Because Hedberg was still wearing his mask with a large moose painted on it, Penguins fans immediately started "mooing" him (not booing), giving him the instant nickname of "Moose." During a game, his superstition begins as soon as he freezes the puck to stop play. He cradles the puck in his glove and must flip it three times before handing it over to the linesman.

BRYAN HELMER: *Tells a Good Story*

In his fifteen years of pro hockey, Bryan Helmer dressed for many teams and leagues, only 134 games' worth of which occurred in the NHL. His craziest season was certainly 1998–99 when he played for four teams (Las Vegas, Phoenix, St. Louis, and Worcester) in three leagues (the IHL, NHL, and AHL).

Although he is a bit superstitious, he also tells a better story about a teammate who, unfortunately, remains unnamed. "I played with a goalie who had this box," he related one time. "It had Billy Smith's picture on the front of it. He had the box locked. No one knew what it was. He always carried it around, was always holding it before games. So one day he was out on the ice, and the guys broke into it. There was a horseshoe in it."

Helmer's own superstition pales by comparison but is odd nonetheless. Never a coffee drinker, he once had half a cup before a game and played well. Ever since he has kept to his regimen of half a cup before every game, even though he never takes a sip of coffee any other time during the year. "That's the only time I ever drink it, before games," he admits.

PAUL HENDERSON: *Even Heroes Believe*

Paul Henderson, the hero of the Summit Series in 1972, was a member of the Toronto Maple Leafs during the years immediately before and after he scored the greatest goal in hockey history. He played from 1967 to 1974 with the Blue and White before leaving to join the WHA and sign with the local Toros.

Henderson always drove to Maple Leaf Gardens for games and practice, but he refused to drive up Yonge Street, which would have been the easiest route for him. One time Henderson and his wife had visitors in town, and they wanted to drive up Yonge Street to see the sights along the world's longest road on their way to the game. The Leafs lost both games. "So now we drive up Church Street whether we're taking out-of-town people to the game or not," he admitted.

RON HEXTALL: Smack, Boom, Bang!

Perhaps the most exciting goalie ever to play in the NHL, Ron Hextall was the third generation of Hextall to play in the league, following his grandfather, Bryan, and father, Bryan Jr. Ron was famous not as much for big saves as he was for two lesser aspects of the position that he turned into essential parts of his repertoire—handling the puck and physical pugnacity.

Perhaps these were characteristics he honed because he hated being caged in his crease, like any goalie historically had been. He was itchy and fidgety and hated to see a puck roll along the boards on a shoot-in while he just watched it from the blue ice. Hextall practised his shot every day and could fire the puck from his goal crease over the glass at the far end, a testament to his great shot and wrist strength.

By the time he retired in 1999, he had scored two goals and was far and away the career leader in penalty minutes among goalies with 714, a total few skaters have attained. On December 8, 1987, Hextall became the first goalie to fire the puck into the (empty) net in a game, and a year and a half later he replicated the feat in the playoffs. He also had three straight years of at least one hundred penalty minutes, a record surely set to last decades.

Hextall was also the first goalie to keep a water bottle on top of his goal, and, as part of his herky-jerky nature, during every stoppage in play he went through a series of gestures to ensure his correct position in the crease. Assuming his place in front of the net, he would bang each post several times with his stick to make sure he was square to the goal, a superstition he maintained to ensure confidence in his positioning.

He also can claim a variation to the "drive the same route to the arena every day" superstition. Hextall went one further and had to drive at the same speed when he got to a particular point of his drive.

DALE HUNTER: Lucky Horse Blanket

One tough and unpopular hombre, Dale Hunter was as soft-spoken off ice as he was hard-edged on it. He is the only player in NHL history with 300 goals and 3,000 penalty minutes to his credit (323 and 3,565, to be exact), and he took longer to get to 1,000 points (1,308 games) than any other player in the 1,000-point club.

And therein lies the paradox. Violent, suspended several times, he was also a scorer and offensive star who recorded at least twenty goals in a season nine times. He was suspended for twenty-one games during the 1993 playoffs for a vicious crosscheck to Pierre Turgeon's back while Turgeon was celebrating a goal. Yet Hunter is also the only player in NHL history to score two overtime goals in the final game of a playoff series.

Hunter's superstition involved a black-and-white sports jacket that he wore faithfully to the arena every game he played, regardless of the weather. Teammates called it the horse blanket, but Hunter wore it without fail and the coat/blanket, in turn, gave him 19 years and 1,407 regular-season games in the NHL.

"PUNCH" IMLACH: The Fearful Dictator

No general manager or coach during the Original Six era was more feared than "Punch" Imlach. Players had no union, no power, no leverage. They were told when to play, with what team, and at what salary, and if they didn't like it, there were many like-skilled replacements in the AHL waiting for a chance to play in the NHL.

Imlach was famous for sending players to the minors as a way to scare them and the entire team, but he was also compassionate at times. Yet for all his bravura and power, he was a deeply superstitious coach who lived virtually every moment of his life with some higher—or magical—purpose in mind.

If the Leafs won a game, he'd do everything the same way the next game, not just talk to the same people but touch the same doorknobs and walk the same way. He always wore the same suit after a win. He would buy a new suit in Montreal at Tony

Few people in hockey were as superstitious as Toronto's "Punch" Imlach, coach of the team's four Stanley Cup teams in the 1960s.

the Tailor's before the Leafs played the Canadiens. If the team won, he'd buy another suit there on his next visit. If not, Tony would lose a sale.

He had a lucky hat, and even its position on his head was important. Pushed down over his head meant that things were going poorly; pushed back, he was happy and the team was winning. Hats on a bed were not allowed. He never carried a two-dollar bill in his pocket.

Most noticeable of all, though, was his love of the number 11. He liked his favourite rookie to wear that number, which is how Gilbert Perreault wore it in Buffalo. Imlach had moved on to coach the expansion Sabres, and they selected the fast-skating forward with the first selection at the 1970 Entry Draft. Imlach insisted Perreault wear number 11, and the player went on to a Hall of Fame career.

GARY INNESS: Just Relax

A goalie with limited staying power in the NHL in the 1970s, Gary Inness played eight years of pro hockey with Pittsburgh, Philadelphia, and Washington as well as stints in the AHL and WHA. Most famously, he was the number-one goalie for the Penguins in 1974–75 when the team made it to the second round of the playoffs. They led the New York Islanders 3–0 in their best-of-seven series but went on to lose in seven games, only the second team after the 1942 Detroit Red Wings to blow a three-game lead in a playoff series.

Inness had a pre-game–night superstition of going to a movie and then to Howard Johnson's for a chocolate sundae. While even a goalie today might understand the comfort of taking in a flick, no goalie would be caught scarfing down a boatload of calories during the season, let alone the night before playing a big game. Nonetheless, it was all part of Inness's ritual, and it worked for him—for a while anyway.

QUICKSHOT JAROMIR JAGR

Jaromir Jagr was one of the most feared scorers during his heyday with the Pittsburgh Penguins, with whom he won the Art Ross Trophy five times, but few opponents knew of his superstition, which would have made for great trash-talking material during games. The night before playing, Jagr liked to have a glass of milk and cookies to settle him down.

PETR KLIMA: One and Done

Finding just the right stick is a difficult—some players would say impossible—task, especially for the scoring stars of the game. Perhaps the defensive defenceman could play with any kind of stick in his hands, but the sniper needs a carefully crafted instrument created exactly to his specifications.

The perfect stick must be the right length, have the right feel and be of the perfect weight, and offer a favoured curve to the blade. The lie must be exact. Everything about a stick's composition is important to a player's confidence in his or her ability to put the puck in the net, as it were. If a stick isn't just so, players can feel as if they're using a club instead of a work of finely sculpted art.

And beyond the general makeup of a stick, any player from Friday-night shinny to *Hockey Night in Canada* will tell you that some sticks have a lot of goals in them and others have none. The former are the ones you tape and retape, glue together however you must to keep them intact until you bleed every last goal from its generous blade.

Not so, however, for Czech star Petr Klima. He defected to the NHL in 1985 and won a Stanley Cup with Edmonton in 1989–90, but his stick theory was just the opposite of the norm. He believed that every stick had exactly *one* goal in it, no more, no less. As a result, every time he scored he would return to the bench, break the stick, and get a new one from the rack.

In his estimation, he would score that next goal faster with a new stick than by expecting his old one to offer up yet another goal. One and done was Klima's rule of thumb.

GUY LAPOINTE: *Messing with a Superstition*

There are two fairly common elements of player superstitions. One, they are silly, insane, ridiculous, personal, unique, important. Two, because every player has them, there is an unwritten rule not to mess with the superstitions of others. After all, they are intended to help a player play better, so as a teammate why would you do anything to tamper with that?

Of course, for every rule there has to be one exception, and in this case it is Guy Lapointe, the resident practical joker of the Montreal Canadiens for many years. And what better stage to mess with a superstition than the 1976 Canada Cup, when many of his teammates for the short tournament were not his teammates for the year-long rigours of the NHL?

The victim was Phil Esposito, only one of the greatest scorers in the game's history. "Espo" loved a particular pair of flip-flops. He wore them into the shower every day after practice, every night after a game. He would not shower without this specific pair. Well, after one Team Canada practice, Lapointe got to the dressing room first and taped said valued flip-flops with what must have been miles of tape. "Espo" got back to the room, couldn't find his beloved footwear, and guessed the hunk of tape that lay in their place were his flippies. He spent the next hour unwinding the tape and cursing, while his teammates watched the entertainment gleefully. Fortunately, Canada won the inaugural Canada Cup.

GEORGE LARAQUE: *Here a Bump, There a Bump*

When he was a member of the Montreal Canadiens, George became *Georges* and Laraque remained the native Montrealer's good old French-Canadian name. But before he came home to play, Laraque was with the Pittsburgh Penguins for a year and a half. Although he wasn't around when the team won the Stanley Cup in June 2009, Laraque made his presence felt on the ice and off.

On ice, Laraque was one of the top fighters in the game. Euphemistically, that meant he was a team player, a fourth liner, a forward who had to hustle every shift. In practical terms, it meant he was out there to protect the team's stars and make sure the opposition didn't get too physical with the likes of Sidney Crosby, Evgeni Malkin, and Jordan Staal.

Off ice, Laraque has a superstitious sequence of bumps and thumps with the trainers and equipment staff before going on the ice. On his way from the dressing room, Laraque had to tap the helpers in a particular order—Scott Adams, Brett Hart, Paul DeFazio, then Dana Heinze. Once, when Heinze forgot the drill, Laraque found him in his office and gave him a good-luck bump there—and only then could he skate onto the ice.

STÉPHAN LEBEAU: *Game Day by the Clock*

Stéphan Lebeau began his career with the Montreal Canadiens, a dream come true for any Quebecker. Not big, but fleet of foot, Lebeau was a scorer at every level he played. In the Quebec Major Junior Hockey League, for instance, he finished his career in Shawinigan, scoring ninety-four goals and a like number of assists in only sixty-seven games. In his first three full seasons with the Canadiens, he had goal totals of twenty-two, twenty-seven, and thirty-one in 1992–93, the year the Habs last won the Stanley Cup.

Despite showing signs of becoming a super-star, Lebeau tailed off badly, was traded, and soon found himself on the outside of the NHL looking in. He made his way to Europe and played another six years in Switzerland.

Wherever he went, Lebeau had a particular game-day series of activities, some that might fall under the rubric of preparation, others without question superstitions. He woke up at 8:30 a.m. to have a breakfast of oatmeal, two slices of bread, orange juice, and a glass of milk. After the morning skate, he'd come home, have a hamburger, watch television, and sleep for an hour and a half. Four hours before the game, he'd have a plate of spaghetti for carbs, and two and a half hours before the game he'd arrive at the arena. He chewed twenty to twenty-five pieces of gum, taped his sticks, and then went to the sauna for just a few minutes. Then he'd dress and be ready to play.

PELLE LINDBERGH: Pripps, Please

After playing for Sweden at the 1980 Olympics, goalie Pelle Lindbergh embarked on a pro career in North America that saw him rise quickly from the AHL to NHL, with Philadelphia. Once with the Flyers, he again rose to prominence, taking the team to the Stanley Cup finals in 1985, where Philly lost to the dynastic Edmonton Oilers.

But a career that had nothing but hope and promise ahead ended horrifically the night of November 10, 1985, when Lindbergh smashed his Porsche into a wall at high speed, sustaining fatal injuries. His blood alcohol was measured to be 0.24 per cent, nearly two and a half times New Jersey's state limits of 0.1 per cent. He was twenty-six years old.

Lindbergh's superstitions included two noteworthy additions to the library of odd and crazy. He wore the same orange T-shirt he had brought with him from Sweden for every game, a freebie from a sporting good manufacturer back home. Whenever the shirt sustained a rip, he'd have it repaired. But it was that shirt or nothing for the goalie.

Between every period, he had to drink a Swedish beverage called Pripps. It had to be served in a cup and have two ice cubes, and it had to be delivered to him by the same trainer. If both of these rules were not adhered to, he wouldn't drink it.

DOUG MACLEAN: *Four-Leaf Clover*

While most people might thank their lucky stars for the good fortune of having coached in the NHL, Doug MacLean can thank his lucky key chain instead.

After coaching university hockey in New Brunswick, MacLean landed a pro gig with Baltimore in the AHL in 1990. He was successful and landed the head coaching job of the young Florida Panthers in the summer of 1995.

In his first season, MacLean managed to take the team to the Stanley Cup finals, only to lose to Detroit in a four-game sweep. It was a stunning success, but things went downhill from there. A year later, the team was eliminated in the first round of the play-offs, and early into his third season he was fired.

Still, that first season in Florida was special, and MacLean attributes his good fortune to an act of kindness and support. While the team was in New York during a bad stretch, a fan game him a four-leaf clover key chain. That night, the visiting Panthers beat the Rangers, and MacLean kept the lucky charm with him the rest of the year—all the way to the Stanley Cup finals.

KEITH MAGNUSON: Green Means Go, and Green Means Win

Keith Magnuson was one of the toughest, fiercest competitors ever to play hockey. He stood up for his teammates, blocked shots with his jaw, and played defence like a rock. He played only 589 career games—all with Chicago—but he fought tooth and nail for and during every minute he was on ice.

Magnuson had two superstitions in particular to which he had to adhere. First, he had to be the second player on the ice, after his goalie. It was his way of getting into the game as quickly as possible.

Second, he and Cliff Koroll always drove to the games together and always took the same route. But that wasn't enough. They also wanted to get every green light along Ogden Avenue. "We'd be creeping along, trying to hit it when it would turn green," Magnuson once confessed. "We'd have cars honking at us, but we thought that if we could get through all those lights that we'd definitely win that night."

They weren't always right, but they were right often enough to make it to the Stanley Cup finals twice, in 1971 and 1973, only to lose to Montreal on both occasions.

EVGENI MALKIN: Playing Footsie

When a player is as talented as Evgeni Malkin, it doesn't take long for him to fit into a team and become a key element in its success. It also makes him a popular player among fans and teammates alike, which is why his very Russian first name has been North Americanized to Gino.

In his four years in the NHL, all with the Pittsburgh Penguins, Malkin has become one of the "big three" in the league alongside teammate Sidney Crosby and compatriot Alexander Ovechkin of the Washington Capitals. All three have now won the Art Ross Trophy, and the two Penguins stars led their team to Stanley Cup victory in the spring of 2009.

One night, Malkin discovered a good-luck superstition quite by accident. Just as he skated off the ice at the end of warm-up, he shot a puck lightly off the foot of trainer Chris Stewart. Malkin had a good game, and the next night he expected Stewart to be in position for another puck off the foot. Stewart wasn't there; Malkin got mad; and the rest is history.

Stewart is always the last man off the ice because he wants to make sure no player is injured. Malkin likes being the last off—another superstition—and the puck bounce off the trainer's foot is now standard fare before every game. "Whatever works for him works for me," Stewart commented. "If that's what he wants, why not do it? I'm not going to screw with anybody's ritual. If I can help him play better, so be it."

CESARE MANIAGO and the Lucky Sock

By the time the ancient warrior of the goal crease arrived in Vancouver to play his final two seasons

(1976–78) of a distinguished seventeen-year NHL career, Cesare (pronounced Caesar, as in "Hail, Caesar!," his nickname) Maniago had his superstitions down to a T. When he began with the Toronto Maple Leafs in 1960, he was a barefaced Original Six goalie, and by the time he retired, he was wearing a mask and staring at an eighteen-team league bloated beyond recognition from his childhood.

Maniago was careful about many details on game day. He selected his clothing based on its effect the previous game, refusing to wear something he lost in on anther night. He always arrived at the arena early to ensure getting his lucky parking spot, and then in the dressing room he had to decide which foot deserved his lucky sock, the sock with two holes in it.

He'd put the sock on his left foot if he won with it last time, but if he lost the sock went on his right foot. The sock alternated feet, back and forth, but one foot or another, the sock always went on. "Having superstitions eases the mind," he said during his days with the Canucks. "You kind of figure if you've done everything exactly right beforehand, nothing much can go wrong when you're on the ice."

QUICK SHOT "MUSH" MARCH

"Mush" March had two notable firsts to his credit. As a member of the Chicago Black Hawks, he scored the first goal in the history of Maple Leaf Gardens, the night of November 12, 1931. Three years later, he became the first NHLer to score an overtime goal to win the Stanley Cup, a feat he also achieved with the Hawks. Fittingly, March's superstition required him to be the first to open the players' gate and skate onto the ice. Even when he was injured, he'd be at the door, with crutches, to open the door before any of his healthy, playing teammates. Wally Kilrea, on the other hand, another player from the 1930s, had to be the last player to leave the dressing room.

JOHN MCINTYRE: *Alpha and Omega*

John McIntyre led perhaps the most superstitious life of any player. He played for four teams in the 1990s for a total of 351 games, his longest stint coming with the Los Angeles Kings (three years and 178 games).

"It was unbelievable," Kings teammate Luc Robitaille once said of him. "From the moment he arrives at the arena until he's back in the hotel, everything he does is a superstition." Of course, he had a certain way of dressing and did things at certain times, but the oddest was one of the last. "I remember," Robitaille said with a laugh, "after every game he'd come off the ice and get undressed, and he'd fold his dirty underwear so it looked like when it was clean before the game."

KYLE MCLAREN: *Clueless in San Jose*

If you don't have thick skin, can't take a joke at your own expense, and can't endure being laughed at, an NHL dressing room is not the place for you. For about three years, defenceman Kyle McLaren wore a yellow visor, the result of a joke that became a superstition.

He played the first seven years of his career with the Boston Bruins (1995–2002) and then was traded to the San Jose Sharks before the 2002–03 season after a contract dispute with the Bruins. He was known more for his hard hitting and defensive play than his scoring from the blue line, but he was always a valuable asset to any team's corps of defencemen.

The yellow visor began as a joke. McLaren is colour blind, so before one game players changed his clear visor to a yellow one. He didn't notice until someone asked him about it after the game, but he scored the winning goal that night and decided to keep it on. It stood him in good stead until late in the 2007–08 season when he reverted to the clear version in an attempt to change the team's playoff fortunes.

In recent years, the Sharks have had plenty of Stanley Cup–quality talent but have never made it very far in the playoffs. McLaren's change of visor didn't help, however, as the team lost in six games to the Dallas Stars in the second round of the 2008 playoffs, another early exit for the team after another 100-point season (their third in four years—they had 99 in 2005–06).

SAMMY MCMANUS: No Number 13, No Matter What

A forward from between the wars, Sammy McManus played only briefly with the Montreal Maroons and the Boston Bruins in a career that consisted of mostly minor-league play. Although he was born in Ireland, he was raised in Canada and helped Montreal's "English" team win the Stanley Cup in his only full season, 1934–35. Besides that, and one game with the Bruins, McManus played in the AHL and its predecessors, the CAHL and IAHL (the former standing for Can–Am, the latter International–American Hockey League).

If the number 13 still holds superstitious value in the twenty-first century, it's difficult to imagine just how obsessive people were about the number seventy years ago when talismans and religious values were far more ingrained in the communal psyche. Indeed, McManus dreaded the number so much that he would never go on the ice behind a player who wore a sweater number that, combined with his own, added up to thirteen. Now that's caution.

QUICK SHOT GILLES MELOCHE

Gilles Meloche was an NHL goalie for seventeen years (1971–88), albeit often with dreadful teams (California Golden Seals, Cleveland Barons). He later became the number-one man for the Minnesota North Stars for seven years (1978–85), making the playoffs all but the first season. Wherever he played he was consistent in one regard: he always wore a headband during games. He changed it after every period in which he played poorly and kept it on if he had played well.

MARK MESSIER: Don't Worry

Mark Messier remains the only man to captain two different teams to the Stanley Cup. That's not surprising given that he is often called the finest leader the game has known. An important part of Messier's character was his ability to say and do the right thing at the right time. As such, he refused to rely on luck and is possibly the only player not to have any superstitions—he hated them. He relied on his own abilities, his own motivation from within, to succeed. No rabbit's feet or lucky T-shirt needed for the "Moose."

He gave the greatest example of his un-superstitious-like qualities on May 25, 1994. It was the playoffs, and Messier and the New York Rangers were trailing the New Jersey Devils 3–2 in a best-of-seven series. The Devils were the home team for game six. After practice, the day before the game, Messier told reporters: "We know we have to win it. We can win it. And we are going to win it." The morning of the game, newspapers across New York made headlines of his "guaranteed win."

Any player will admit that no one should ever make a promise like this. It only serves to motivate the other team and makes the chances of delivering the goods on such a promise slim to none. Better keep quiet. Not Messier.

For a while, though, it looked like he was going to be made a fool of. The Devils jumped into a 2–0 lead early in the first and continued to lead by that score late in the second. Then Messier fed Alex Kovalev the puck on a two-on-one, and with one quick shot it was a 2–1 game after two periods.

With twenty minutes left in the Rangers' season and trailing by a goal, Messier took control. He scored early in the third period to tie the game, 2–2, and midway through he got to a rebound first, beat goalie Martin Brodeur, and put his team up, 3–2. Late in the game, playing four-on-six because of a penalty and an empty New Jersey net, Messier stole the puck in his own end and fired it into the open cage to complete the hat trick and seal a guaranteed win. The Rangers went on to win game seven—and the Stanley Cup for the first time since 1940—proving that heroes and heroic play do not require superstitions.

STAN MIKITA: *Butt, Of Course*

The good old days are so called because they were very good, indeed, and because they occurred a long

Chicago players make their way down the stairs from the ice to the dressing room. Mikita always enjoyed a final puff of his cigarette on the walk up to ice level.

time ago. The superstition of Hall of Famer Stan Mikita is from an era long gone and a time long past, yet it evokes that era and time so perfectly that we are thankful to have had such a superstition to chronicle.

First, a bit of history is required. Mikita played every one of his 22 seasons and 1,394 regular-season games with Chicago, facts alone that attest to the good old days. He is also one of a small group of players to have skated in the NHL in four decades, having made his debut in 1959 and retired in 1980.

In his era, many players smoked socially, and many among that group enjoyed a mischievous puff in the toilet during intermissions. It was not uncommon to look into the bathroom of the dressing room and see the door closed, skates on the floor, and plumes of smoke rising from behind.

Now, another interesting feature of the era was the Chicago Stadium. It had a loud pipe organ to urge fans to clap and cheer on the hometown Black Hawks, and it also had a strange architectural feature in that stairs led players from the ice down to their dressing rooms. Almost as soon as they left the playing surface, they'd have to walk down a flight of stairs in skates.

These back stories explain Mikita's superstition. He liked to have a cigarette in the corridor leading to the ice before every period, and just as he started to climb the stairs he'd toss the butt over his left shoulder. In this way did he feel relaxed and ready to play the next period of hockey.

ALFIE MOORE: Hat/No Hat

In a fifteen-year professional career, Alfie Moore played in only twenty-one NHL games, none more memorable than one night in 1938 when he played

Goalie Alfie Moore was superstitious about wearing a hat—and then not wearing one after he lost it.

for the Chicago Black Hawks in the Stanley Cup playoffs.

The Hawks were in Toronto to play the Leafs on the night of April 5, 1938, but their regular goalie, Mike Karakas, had a toe injury and couldn't play. With only hours to go until the opening faceoff, the Hawks scrambled to find any local goalie of skill, and as legend has it they found Moore in a bar. Although that part of the story is up for discussion, Moore's incredible play in leading Chicago to a 3–1 win that night at Maple Leaf Gardens is not. Gordie Drillon scored first for the Leafs at 1:53, but that was the only goal Moore surrendered. The Hawks went on to win the Cup, and Moore got his name on the bowl for this one masterful game.

Most of the rest of his career passed quietly with a variety of teams in the minors. Moore, like many a player in the early days, wore a hat when he played. Sometimes players wore them to keep their heads warm at a time when arenas were cold, and others wore them for vanity. Aurèle Joliat, for instance, wore one because he was prematurely bald.

But once when he was playing in Montreal, Moore couldn't find his small cap and had to play bare-headed. He posted a shutout that night and never wore a hat again. One superstition quickly reversed simply because of a win.

JUSTIN MORNEAU: Roy's Biggest Fan

If there is a non-hockey player whose superstitions belong with the skaters of the ice lanes it is baseball star Justin Morneau. A native of British Columbia and the son of two athletic parents, Morneau was a goalie for as long as he was a first baseman in his years leading up to a career in Major League Baseball. He went so far as to earn a spot as the third goalie for the Portland Winter Hawks before finally giving up hockey to focus on baseball, a wise decision given that he went on to become the first Canadian to be named the American League's most valuable player, in 2006.

As a kid, regardless of whether it was baseball or hockey, Morneau worshipped the number 33 because his hero was Montreal Canadiens goalie Patrick Roy. Yes, Morneau wears that number today with the Minnesota Twins, but years ago he went to even greater extremes. When his dad would drive him to hockey games, Justin wouldn't get out of the car until the car clock read, for instance, 6:33.

Morneau's love of the number 33 is strictly a Roy honour and has nothing to do with Larry Walker, another Canadian who started out playing hockey and who wore number 33 during his career.

Walker was simply a "3 freak," as it were, and controlled his life around that lucky number. But that's another story.

LOU NANNE: *Same As It Ever Was*

Lou Nanne was the Minnesota North Stars general manager from 1978 to 1988, during which time he not only maintained his own superstitions but imposed them on the team.

Nanne would sit in the press box and not move a muscle so long as the team was winning, but if they were losing, he'd get up and find a new chair, circle it four times, and sit down. Repeat until successful. He also wore the same clothes to keep a win streak going and did everything the same day after day so long as the team was doing well. A loss changed everything.

As for the players, they were forced, in many ways, to follow along, as Brian Bellows, one of the stars, revealed. "If we'd win, we'd stay in the same hotel, eat the same food, wear the same jerseys, use the same bus driver, leave at the same time. He'd drive you crazy," Bellows said of his general manager.

RICK NASH: *Too Many, Too Private*

Like many a player, Columbus Blue Jackets captain Rick Nash is too superstitious to go into many details about his routine, but his life is full of effort to improve his luck. For starters, he dresses left to right when there are two like pieces of equipment to put on. Also, he has to be first on the ice, even before the goalie, which is an oddity, to be sure. Lastly, he also takes the same number of shots during every pre-game skate.

Beyond that, he won't reveal much, but given that he's one of the league's purest goal-scorers and a frequent representative for Team Canada (most recently at the gold-medal-winning Olympics in Vancouver in February 2010), he has every right to be quiet about his superstitions.

BERNIE NICHOLLS: *"Pumper-Nicholl" and Twig*

How many players' goal celebrations are given nicknames? Bernie Nicholls had such an exuberant and distinct act after putting the puck in the net—coupled with his name—that his earned a moniker.

After a goal, he'd take the stick in his left hand, lift his right leg parallel to the ground, and pump his right arm back and forth. That's how the "Pumper-Nicholl" got its name (although the celebration is something he had been doing, unnamed, since he was a kid).

And the "Pumper-Nicholl" was often seen in Los Angeles, where he played for nine years, especially in 1988–89 when he had a career year in scoring. That season in Nicholls's stats panel sticks out like a sore thumb—70 goals, 80 assists, 150 total points. Only one other time did he reach 100 points (1984–85, when he had exactly 100), and this incredible season can be explained by two words: (1) Wayne and (2) Gretzky. You see, they were linemates, and as anyone who ever played with number 99 will attest, all you have to do is keep your stick on the ice, be ready for a pass, and you'll score more than you've ever scored before.

Still, Nicholls had 475 career goals over 18 NHL seasons and six teams. With or without Gretzky, that's a lot of "Pumper-Nicholls." And like many a scorer, his stick was the centre of his superstition, but surely his is particularly noteworthy.

On game days, Nicholls kept his stick with him at all times. This is a literal description. He took it home with him after the morning skate, kept it by the table as he had his meal, took it to bed with him for his pre-game nap. "All times" means, incredibly, just that.

QUICKSHOT JOE NIEUWENDYK

Joe Nieuwendyk knows a thing or two about hockey. He won the Stanley Cup with three different teams in three different decades (Calgary Flames, 1989; Dallas Stars, 1999; New Jersey Devils, 2003), and retired with 564 goals and 1,126 total points to his credit. So his game-day preparations must be respected. Indeed, Nieuwendyk always ate two pieces of peanut buttered–toast before each game. This big-kid superstition enabled him to post fifteen seasons of twenty goals or more.

BOBBY ORR: Even the Greatest Make Believe

Who would have thought that the greatest player of all time would have a superstition that, quite frankly, stinks? But that's the case with Bobby Orr, the defenceman who revolutionized the game, the man whose skating was poetry and whose courage was unequalled, the man who gave his body to the game until there was nothing left to give.

Few players taped their stick as idiosyncratically as Bobby Orr.

By the time he retired in 1978, his knees had been so ravaged by surgeries he couldn't walk up a flight of stairs. Orr is the only defenceman to win the Art Ross Trophy (a trick he turned twice), and his offensive abilities from the blue line were the stuff of legend. Because he scored so frequently, his superstition is all the more putrid. He liked to wear the same hockey socks—unwashed—until he didn't score a goal.

Orr also had to touch every player before a game. In the dressing room, he'd walk around and pat each teammate on the shoulder or arm for good luck.

He had another habit that might be considered superstition or strategic, depending on interpretation. He taped his stick in singular fashion to any other player in the game's history, using only one strand of black tape a few inches from the toe of the blade. This single strand acted as a mark the way an X on a stage would indicate where an actor should stand for a particular scene. The strand helped Orr position the puck when he stickhandled or shot, and it gave him a reference on an otherwise vacant stick.

While every other player in the game taped his stick fully from toe to heel, Orr didn't like so much material coming between his stick and the puck. In part, this was superstition. After all, had he played with a fully taped stick one can be sure he would have been just as great a player. On the other hand, there is a strategy to his stick taping that makes practical sense, too.

MIKE PALMATEER: *The Popcorn Kid*

One of the most popular goalies in the post–Original Six of the Toronto Maple Leafs, Mike Palmateer was quirky and exciting, fun-loving and entertaining. He also happened to be an excellent goalie until knee injuries forced him to retire at age thirty.

Everything about Palmateer was fun. He wore a series of masks in blue and white that were engaging for their design. He flopped and dived in his crease

Mike Palmateer enjoyed popcorn before games.

like a ballerina or a drunk, depending on whether or not his acrobatic efforts kept the puck out of the net. Everything he did looked a little awkward because he was small and caught with his right hand. He was loved by fans and teammates, and was part of the teams of 1978 and 1979, when the Leafs came closest to getting back to the Stanley Cup finals.

Palmateer also sported curly hair and this, combined with his love of eating popcorn before a game, earned him the nickname "The Popcorn Kid." Popcorn never was known as a stimulant or an effective food group to aid a goalie's performance, but it was his belief that a few kernels before the game would help him play better.

BERNIE PARENT: Phantom of the Crease

The 1960s was an era of tremendous change. Of course, the NHL expanded from six to twelve teams, and to fourteen in 1970, but it was also the decade when almost all goalies switched from playing barefaced to wearing a mask. While the improved safety was beyond reproach, masks did make one startling change to the drama of watching a game.

In the mask-less days, fans could see a goalie's every expression, how he grimaced to reach for a puck, how he played in pain after getting hit by a shot, how he cringed after allowing a goal. The goalie's face was pure theatre, offering fans the full range, from comedy to drama. Once they donned the masks, these expressions were hidden forever.

In thespian terms, however, one might say goalies went from being theatre in the round to kabuki. They decorated their masks with images that hopefully inspired fear in enemy shooters or intimidated the opposition in some way. They reflected the team's colours or the goalie's personality. From being utterly conspicuous, a goalie's expressions became inscrutable.

This was just how Philadelphia Flyers goalie Bernie Parent liked it. He didn't like anyone associated with the game—fans, officials, opponents—to see his face at any time. So, from the moment he got up from his stall in the dressing room to hit the ice until the time he returned to said stall, he kept his mask firmly on his face, giving him the unknowable character that, he believed, played on the minds of his opponents.

QUICKSHOT COREY PERRY

Anaheim Ducks forward Corey Perry has quickly developed into one of the finest young players in the NHL, as a scorer, playmaker, and leader (not to mention a member of Canada's Olympic gold team from Vancouver in February 2010). An energetic personality, he likes to tap everything on the way out the dressing room to the ice. He taps the wall and the door and whatever else he can find that brings him good luck.

QUICKSHOT JACQUES PLANTE

Jacques Plante was not only an innovator and a pioneer, he was also one of the quirkiest goalies in a profession that is the very dictionary definition of the word *quirky*. One of his habits to relax was knitting, a grandmotherly trait he was not shy about. He believed that if he wore underwear that he himself knitted, he'd play better. And he alone could wash said underwear. If someone else did, that person would wash the luck right out of the undergarments. Not good for a Hall of Fame goalie.

QUICKSHOT FÉLIX POTVIN

Félix Potvin made his NHL debut in 1991–92 and became the star goalie for a generation of Leafs fans before being traded early in the 1998–99 season. "The Cat" made a cross out of tape and put it on his stall before every game. Was this born of a Catholic upbringing in rural Quebec? A hockey prayer and Hail Mary's–worth of good luck? Potvin wouldn't say, but it's certainly an odd means of asking God to watch over him.

QUICKSHOT STÉPHANE QUINTAL

Stéphane Quintal was a sixteen-year NHL defenceman with six teams, his longest stay coming in his home province with the Montreal Canadiens. He had the unusual superstition of never speaking to anyone after 1:30 p.m. on the day of a game. No doubt the anti-social habit was off-putting for some teammates and members of the coaching staff and media, but it gave him 1,037 regular-season games, so he had no reason to change.

CRAIG RAMSAY: Two to Be Good

In a career that lasted 1,070 regular season games and fourteen years, all with the Buffalo Sabres, defenceman Craig Ramsay was around long enough to adopt and ditch several superstitions, but the number 2 always seemed to play a role in his game-day mentality, particularly during the pre-game skate.

Ramsay made a habit of leaving the ice with exactly two minutes left on the clock for the warm-up, and before he left he had to take two shots, one from the centre red line, the second from the blue line. Teammate Ric Seiling was aware of this super-stition and made sure to get Ramsey the pucks needed for the shots. Then, when it was time to head from the dressing room to the ice to start the game, Ramsay was the second-last player to leave.

Like all players, he'd do a final few laps casually, and like most players he finished with the goalie. At that point, he'd stop in front of his 'tender, tap the ice twice, and then tap his pads twice before skating to the blue line for the national anthem.

QUICKSHOT BILL RANFORD

Much like Johan Hedberg a generation later, long-time Edmonton goalie Bill Ranford had the same routine every time he froze the puck for a faceoff. He had to flip the puck in the air and have it land on the back of his catcher before giving it to the linesman.

"CHICO" RESCH: Baby, Don't You Drive That Car

Glen Resch earned the nickname "Chico" for his resemblance—at least in the eyes of Islanders teammate Doug Rombough—to the eponymous character in the 1970s television show *Chico and the Man*. Resch played the first eight years of his career with the Islanders (1973–81), winning the Stanley Cup in 1980 and 1981. Small and popular, he was often the number-one goalie, although, he split a healthy number of games with his backup, Billy Smith.

Resch owned a brown 1937 Dodge Coupe, a car he loved not only to admire but to drive to the arena in. However, he had several bad games after using it, so from then on he left it in the garage on game day. "I've driven that car to games, and things just haven't worked out," he said in reference to his poor play because of the '37 Dodge.

However, if he knows beforehand that he'll be on the bench while Smith plays, Resch will drive in the old antique without hesitation. "It can't hurt the other guy," he deadpanned.

LUC ROBITAILLE: *Tales of the Tape*

"Lucky Luc" Robitaille was the highest-scoring left winger in NHL history. By the time he hung up his skates in 2006, he had recorded 668 goals and 1,394 total points, numbers that will keep him atop the list of left wingers for many years to come. Along the way he had three seasons of at least fifty goals and four seasons of more than one hundred points, and although he played for four teams he is best remembered for his three stints as a member of the Los Angeles Kings.

Robitaille counts two incredibly odd superstitions among the library of curious acts, and he made both an important part of his life not for a few weeks or months but literally his whole career.

He and Tomas Sandstrom were roommates on road trips starting in 1989–90, the first year the two played together in Los Angeles. On the day of one

"Lucky Luc" Robitaille used a stick with white tape for the first and third periods (below) and black tape for the second period (left).

game, Sandstrom checked out of the hotel for the pair, and that night Robitaille had a great game. "You can't ever check out of the hotel again," Sandstrom joked. To which Robitaille said, "Okay" and never did. Never again!

Robitaille also had a particular stick superstition that highlights the somewhat arbitrary nature of tape colour on sticks. If a survey were done, results would probably show more Europeans use white tape and more North Americans use black. Both preferences can be justified.

White tape: By taping the stick white, a player makes it more difficult for an opponent to see the stick itself because it blends in with the ice. At the same time, white tape allows the puck carrier to see the puck on his stick with greater ease.

Black tape: Using tape the colour of the puck allows the stick handler better opportunity to hide the puck because an opponent will have a harder time distinguishing the rubber from the blade. By using tape the opposite colour to the ice surface, a player can also see his stick with greater ease and speed.

Evidently, Robitaille saw merits in both explanations because every game he used sticks with white tape for the first and third periods and black tape for the second period. Did this confuse opponents?

Well, 668 goals suggests goalies were flummoxed, but maybe it was because of his blazing shot more than the colour of tape on his stick.

The superstition came about naturally, though. During one game while he was playing Midget AAA, the team ran out of white tape, his preferred choice. He was forced to make do with black tape for the second period, and as it turned out he played well. For the next quarter of a century, he never deviated from this superstition.

Combined, these are a strange pair of habits, but more unique is that he maintained them for such a long period of time.

PATRICK ROY: Herky-Jerky Quirky

Love him or love to hate him, Patrick Roy, the king of oversized equipment, retired with more wins (551) and games played (1,029) than any other goalie in the NHL's long history. Dubbed "Saint Patrick" after his heroic play in the 1986 Stanley Cup playoffs, he is the only player to win the Conn Smythe Trophy three times, all in Cup-winning performances.

Yet Roy's superstitions seemed to number as many as his career wins. On the ice he considered the goalposts to be his best friends. He talked to them, believing that they were the difference between winning and losing. He was right, of course. A shot off the post can carom into the corner of the rink or the back of the net (as he discovered to his dismay during the shootout at the 1998 Olympics).

Roy also avoided skating over all lines on the ice (i.e., blue lines, red lines), taking a page from long-time Los Angeles Dodgers manager Tommy Lasorda, who never stepped on the chalk between third base and home plate when he paid a visit to a pitcher.

During the pre-game skate, Roy would skate to his blue line and face his net, visualizing it getting smaller and smaller. In the dressing room, he would wind tape around the knob of his stick sixty times (the same number of minutes in a game), and then he'd write the names of his three kids on the shaft.

Needless to say, he dressed in the same order every game, but there's another weird habit as well. During the intermission, he bounced and juggled a puck, and just before the next period began he hid the puck so no one on his team could find it.

That is how you become the winningest goalie in NHL history (that and stopping a lot of pucks).

GEOFF SANDERSON: *The Long and Short of It*

As the only player born in the Northwest Territories ever to play in the NHL, Geoff Sanderson already has a place in the world of hockey history (and trivia). And as a consistent and high-scoring forward, he also left his mark in the league's record books, producing four thirty-goal seasons and two forty-goal seasons. He played more than 1,100 regular-season games, and as a member of the Buffalo Sabres in 1998–99 he played in game seven of the Stanley Cup finals, losing to the Dallas Stars on Brett Hull's controversial, toe-in-the-crease goal in overtime.

Sanderson kept himself game sharp with a very peculiar ritual. He used a different-length stick for

Geoff Sanderson used an ever shorter stick during each period of a game to force himself to bear down and try harder in the face of fatigue.

every period of a game. More specifically, he used an ever shorter stick. For the first period, his stick would be longest; for the second period, it would be about half an inch shorter; for the third, another half-inch shorter.

Sanderson figured that as a game goes on, players get a little tired and, as a result, a little lazy. By making his stick shorter, he forced himself to bear down, hunch over, concentrate just a bit more so he wouldn't have those lapses in performance. Whether the effect was more psychological or physical is something only Sanderson knows, but his seventeen-year career suggests it worked.

QUICK SHOT LAURIE SCOTT

This superstition is difficult to attribute but it's so fantastic it's worth mentioning. Laurie Scott, a player who touched the NHL briefly in the 1920s and 1930s, always had to be the last player to leave the dressing room and always wanted his sticks facing up (i.e., blade in the air, not on the ground). Rumour has it that one day he found the blades of his sticks on the ground and was so incensed he promptly retired from the game right then and there!

EDDIE SHORE: *Feared and Afraid*

One of the best and most feared defencemen of the early game, Eddie Shore once played in the AHL and NHL at the same time, the 1939–40 season, his last as a player. He played all but ten games of his fourteen seasons with Boston, winning his lone Stanley Cup in 1938–39. The Hall of Famer had many a battle with the game's best and toughest opponents, and he was both a supreme player and vicious fighter. For all his genuine talent, Shore was a man of superstitions as much as any teammate or opponent who admired or feared him.

For instance, he would wear only blue shirts on game day. In the dressing room, he had to have a towel over his chair. Most important, though, was his relationship with assistant trainer "Hammy" Moore. Moore had to remove Shore's sweater after every game. The drill was a simple one. Shore would skate off the ice and into the dressing room, extend his arms, and wait for Moore to peel off the sweater. Every game.

QUICKSHOT GARY SIMMONS

Goalie Gary Simmons played in his fair share of leagues and teams. During his eleven seasons, he dressed for a like number of teams in six leagues, which is perhaps why he liked to make a dent on the top of the door to the player's bench at every arena he played in, marking his territory, as it were.

QUICKSHOT CHRIS SIMON

One of the toughest, most penalized, and most often suspended players of the modern era, Chris Simon played for eight teams during his 782-game career. His game-day meal always consisted of a portion and a half of easy-to-make macaroni and cheese for lunch.

QUICKSHOT ALEX SINGBUSH

Defenceman Alex Singbush, who played in the NHL only with the Montreal Canadiens in 1940–41, didn't let anyone touch his shoes.

Current Washington Capitals defenceman Tyler Sloan ratted out a former teammate, without mentioning a name: "I played with a guy that tied his skates before the game in the [toilet]," he explained. "Sat in there on the [toilet], just sat. Closed the lid, sat on the toilet, and tied his skates up in there, every game."

GARY SMITH: *Dressing, Dressing, Dressing Room*

Goalie Gary Smith was nicknamed "Suitcase" because it seemed with the start of every season he was playing on another team. He turned pro in 1964 and retired in 1980, and during that time he played 532 games with seven NHL teams, as well as for teams in the WHA, AHL, WHL, and CPHL (Canadian Professional Hockey League). His longest stay in one place was from 1967 to 1971, when he was with the lowly Oakland/California franchise, which largely explains why he won only 173 games in the big league.

Smith had an odd superstition if ever there was one, especially for a goalie. As any hockey player or hockey lover knows, the goalie has the most equipment and the heaviest padding, and it takes him considerably longer than any other player to get dressed for a game.

Yet Smith not only got dressed before the game; he also undressed, showered, and dressed again during every intermission! Over the course of an evening, that's three complete equipment changes and three showers. Fortunately for him, he retired before overtime became standard during the regular season and he played in only a handful of playoff games (when there was unlimited overtime).

CONN SMYTHE: A Real Screamer

Conn Smythe, the legendary, brilliant owner of the Toronto Maple Leafs, was often nicknamed the "Hollerin' Major" in reference to his rank in the army and his loud voice. That loud voice was never more audible than during games in the 1930s and 1940s when, if "everything goes" wasn't the modus operandi of the NHL, it was certainly omnipresent.

This was an era of wire fencing instead of Plexiglas, an era when brawls would result in just two fighting majors, an era when fans could lean over the dasher to pull the hair of an opposing player. In the case of Smythe, he had a superstition that turned into a strategy. He liked to stand behind the enemy goal, believing the goalie would be intimidated or jinxed by the great man's presence.

Often he was right, and the mighty Leafs would win. When his team didn't score, though, Smythe turned to hollerin' at the goalie through the fence, every word clearly heard by the puckstopper. Whether play was in the far end, when the trash talking was a one-on-one affair, or in the goalie's end, when the goalie had to dissociate himself from the screams as he followed the puck, Smythe harried the poor puckstopper relentlessly.

It was unsettling at best, highly effective at worst for the poor bare-faced goalie. Smythe was a competitor, though, and would use every means in the book to help his team win.

QUICKSHOT DOUG SOETAERT

Goalie Doug Soetaert played in the NHL from the mid-1970s to the mid-1980s with the New York Rangers, Winnipeg Jets, and Montreal Canadiens. He changed his pads between the pre-game skate and start of the first period.

MATS SUNDIN: No Triskaidekaphobia Here

Not surprisingly, the overwhelming majority of NHLers to have worn sweater number 13 are European. And without doubt the finest number 13 of all time is Mats Sundin, who spent most of his career with the Maple Leafs. Sundin and his Euro brethren aren't superstitious about the number at all. Teemu Selanne wore the number at times, but he's considered more of a number 8, and Bill Guerin is probably the best North American to don number 13.

Indeed, go into any high-rise European hotel or apartment building and you'll see a thirteenth floor. In North America, floors jump from the twelfth to the fourteenth so people don't have to "risk" staying on the thirteenth floor. (Some people also refuse to stay on the fourteenth floor because it's really the thirteenth!)

The superstition about number 13 being bad luck comes, in Christianity, at any rate, from the Last Supper, when there were thirteen people at table, one of whom betrayed Jesus. To this day many people will not dine if there are thirteen in a group, and many restaurants will break up a party of thirteen into two smaller groups to avoid the dangerous number.

The greatest number 13 in hockey history, Mats Sundin had no problem wearing the number most North Americans would consider unlucky.

And that's why it never bothered Sundin to wear number 13. Swedish culture has no particular aversion to 13, and he liked the number. Did it work for him? Well, his personal NHL stats would say yes, but he never won the Stanley Cup. Internationally, he might well be regarded as the finest player of the modern era, so any North Americans thinking about wearing number 13 should go ahead and do so—without fear.

MAXIME TALBOT: *Whole Lotta Believin'*

There are two parts to the superstitious activities of Pittsburgh Penguins defenceman Maxime Talbot— game-day events and the final moment before leaving the dressing room to play a game.

On the first count, Talbot's preparations revolve around food. It all begins the night before a game, when he eats the same meal: shrimp cocktail, Caesar salad, Porterhouse steak, and a glass of red wine. The next day at the arena, before the light morning skate, he'll eat cereal and bagels with peanut butter. After the skate and shower, he goes to the same Italian restaurant where he'll have soup, breadsticks, and spaghetti with meat sauce and chicken. With these foods in his system, he can go home, have a nap, and get back to the arena knowing he's ready to play.

He'll get to the rink a couple of hours before a game and go through various lesser rituals, but the moments just before the team heads to the ice to play are critical. He and goalie Marc-André Fleury have a serious series of motions they must go through. Actually, it's more like a quick, friendly sparring session, but as the players line up at the dressing-room door ready for the walk to the ice, Talbot and Fleury give each other a few jabs to get psyched up and ready to rumble, as it were. They did it one night, and Fleury played well, and they've been doing it ever since, their light boxing now a familiar part of Pens' telecasts leading up to the national anthems and opening faceoff.

JOCELYN THIBAULT: Calming Down

It is a remarkable coincidence to be sure that Jocelyn Thibault won the last game ever played at the Montreal Forum *and* the last game at Maple Leaf Gardens. In the case of the former, he was a member of the Canadiens, and in the latter he played for Chicago.

Thibault entered the NHL in 1993 as an eighteen-year-old, a rare accomplishment for a goalie given that puckstoppers usually take longer to mature and often don't make their debut until their early twenties. Thibault started with Quebec/Colorado, but he was the less famous name involved in the trade that sent Patrick Roy to the Avalanche and him to Montreal. In three and a half seasons, though, Thibault wasn't able to replace Roy with the Habs and he was traded to Chicago.

He played briefly with Pittsburgh and Buffalo before retiring at age thirty-two because of a hip injury from which he never fully recovered. In his early days, he admitted to having so many superstitions they almost caused him more anxiety and distraction than they were worth. "I started to think my game relied on my superstitions, which isn't true," he once said. "The game relies on the focus and the effort you put into it. . . . You have to realize [superstitions] are not going to make you good, but they're going to make you comfortable."

Nonetheless, he maintained several throughout his career, namely dressing from right to left when two like pieces of equipment need be applied. During the pre-game skate, he performed the same stretching exercises on the exact same spot on the ice, and between whistles he banged the posts with his stick à la Ron Hextall, the goalie he idolized as a kid.

Strangest of all were the minutes just before he skated onto the ice. He would put his equipment down on the floor in front of him and dress in the same sequence, and then exactly six and a half minutes before he had to skate onto the ice, he poured water on his head.

WAYNE THOMAS: Now That's Quick

One of a small number of goalies to have played for both Toronto and Montreal, Thomas also played parts of four seasons with the New York Rangers during his eight NHL seasons (1972–81; he did not play in 1974–75). He appeared in only four career playoff games, all with the Leafs, and later was an assistant coach in the NHL for several years.

Like any other player, he had a particular way of readying his sticks for puck combat. In his case, he always used black tape, and it had to be from a new roll.

But Thomas also had a unique superstition that helped him get his mind thinking quickly. As players skated around to loosen up before the opening faceoff, they would, of course, come by and tap his pads, pat his head, or give him a short "good game" wish. As they did so, Thomas would speak their names out loud, sometimes having to fire off a series of monikers in rapid succession. That got his tongue working and his brain thinking at the speed he'd need to react when the slapshots started coming toward his cage. Or so he believed.

QUICKSHOT "TINY" THOMPSON

"Tiny" Thompson was a Hall of Fame goalie who starred with the Boston Bruins for most of the 1930s. He is the team's all-time leader in games played, wins, shutouts, and career goals-against average. And like any other goalie, he was superstitious. In his case, he always allowed teammate "Cooney" Weiland to score at the end of the pre-game skate. But if Thompson touched the puck inadvertently on its way into the net, he'd have a bad game. Weiland had to score cleanly for "Tiny" to play well.

QUICKSHOT MARK TINORDI

Mark Tinordi played the better part of twelve seasons in the NHL. The large defenceman didn't have soft hands in the offensive end, but he was one tough hombre inside his own blue line. Yet for all his rough-and-tumble talent, he reverted to childhood on game days, always eating a peanut-butter-and-jelly sandwich on those mornings.

JOHN TONELLI: *A Little Spit*

A winner and competitor through and through, John Tonelli was a four-time Stanley Cup champion and a clutch scorer. Although the records show he had 325 goals in a career that lasted 1,028 regular-season games, it was the timing of his goals, most notably in the playoffs, that mattered more than their volume.

While more obvious stars such as Mike Bossy and Bryan Trottier got most of the attention for the New York Islanders during their dynasty (1980–83), Tonelli made an impact with key plays at key moments, none bigger than his perfect pass to Bob Nystrom for the Cup-winning goal in 1980, the team's first of four championships in a row.

In 1982, the team was losing 3–1 to Pittsburgh in the decisive game. Tonelli assisted on the goal by Mike McEwen to make it 3–2, tied the game himself with two and a half minutes left in regulation, and scored the winner in overtime to send the team on its way to a third Cup win.

Despite being known as a gritty winger who worked hard in the corners, Tonelli was gifted around the net, scoring twenty goals in nine seasons, culminating in 1984–85, when he had forty-two goals and one hundred points. But there was a time when he went into a now-famous scoring slump, only to break out of it, in his mind anyway, when an equipment manager spat on his stick and rubbed the saliva into the blade just before Tonelli went onto the ice. He scored a goal that night, and a superstition was born at the same time a scoring slump was ended.

QUICK SHOT LOUIS TRUDEL

A twenty-year professional beginning in 1932, Louis Trudel always wanted a kid to step on his stick for good luck. It must have worked because he won two Stanley Cups with Chicago, in 1934 and 1938.

DARCY TUCKER: Same Old, Same Old

The erstwhile trash-talkin' fan-lovin' forward of the Toronto Maple Leafs who found new life after joining the Colorado Avalanche, Darcy Tucker is one of only a small group of players to have won the Memorial Cup three times, a feat he achieved with the Kamloops Blazers in 1992, 1994, and 1995.

He began his NHL career with Montreal and Tampa Bay, but he is best remembered for his seven years with the Maple Leafs. He also married Shannon Corson, the sister of teammate Shayne Corson, and the two became fast friends during their mutual years in Toronto.

Tucker was loved and respected because he played a tough game despite being small. He hit hard, played every shift as if it were his last, and drove to the net to create his scoring chances. He went to the middle of the action, not the periphery.

Tucker had plenty of superstitions to keep his mind off the game before the opening faceoff. For starters, he always took the same route to the arena when he was playing well, but as soon as he had a bad game he changed it. Before taking the ice, he drank a concoction made of exactly half-coffee and half-Coke, but if he didn't like the mix he dumped it and created a new one.

On the bench, he always kept the blade of his stick in the air. He used an aluminum shaft with a wooden blade, and he always liked the wood up high in case he had to "knock on wood" for more good luck.

RON TUGNUTT: Move It or Lose It

On March 21, 1991, goalie Ron Tugnutt set a modern-day record by stopping seventy shots in a single game. His Quebec Nordiques managed only a 3–3 tie with Boston, but he had made history. During his seventeen-year NHL career, Tugnutt was both a starting goalie and backup, depending on team and circumstance. His best year was 1998–99, when he led the league with a 1.79 goals-against average and had a record of 22–10–8 in forty-three games.

Perhaps more than any other goalie, he was a man in motion as soon as an official blew the whistle to stop play. Call him fidgety, or ADD, or impatient, he had to be moving all the time. Being stationary drove him nuts, and that, in turn, was not a way to stay focused. Moving around was a constant reminder that he was in the middle of a game.

While some goalies like only to get a drink from their water bottle, Tugnutt wasn't one of them—he didn't keep a water bottle on top of the net like every other goalie did.

Instead, he liked to skate figure eights around the crease up until the last possible second before a faceoff, after which he'd snap into a crouch and get set in the ready position. If the puck were going to be faced off at the far end of the ice, he'd skate out halfway to the blue line, squat, and pop straight up, kicking each pad against his stick and moving his head from side to side. Then he'd raise both arms in the air, touching his stick with his glove. All of these gyrations were intended to keep him loose and focused on the linesman with the puck. No time was idle for Tugnutt.

MARTY TURCO: *What Was He Thinking?*

It's one thing to have a superstition among friends, but to try to maintain one in enemy territory is just plain crazy. The scene was the 2009 playoffs. The teams: the Dallas Stars and the Vancouver Canucks. The series went the distance, seven games, and the Canucks had home ice for the decisive game. That didn't faze Stars goalie Marty Turco.

The night before game five, also in Vancouver, Turco had taken eight teammates out for dinner at a fancy restaurant called Il Giardino. Dallas was trailing 3–1 in the series and had to win the next night to stay alive. The food was excellent, and the next night he posted an overtime shutout as Dallas won 1–0 to get the critical win and stay alive.

The Stars won game six back in Dallas with another Turco shutout, 2–0, and game seven was scheduled two days later back in British Columbia, on a Monday night.

Of course, Turco just had to take the same eight players out to Il Giardino on Sunday night, but the restaurant was closed on Sundays. Turco called and pleaded with the owners, who agreed to open the restaurant just for the players. They sat in the same seats, ate the same food, and drank the same wine. But the next night the Canucks prevailed, 4–1, to win the series and eliminate Dallas. What Turco never knew was that the staff—Canucks fans, of course—had taped a Canucks souvenir coin featuring Vancouver goalie Roberto Luongo underneath Turco's chair. No wonder the Stars lost.

QUICK SHOT ROGIE VACHON

Diminutive goalie Rogie Vachon always took a quick whiff of smelling salts and chewed a piece of gum before heading to the ice for a game to get him going and focused on the task at hand.

STEVE VALIQUETTE: Insane in the Membrane

Everyone knows goalies are crazy. No matter how much protection they wear, they still stand in the way of rubber bullets going more than 160 kilometres an hour. Everyone knows goalies are weird. They like to be left alone, have untold quirks and habits, and are, as the saying goes, a breed unto themselves.

Steve Valiquette takes things even further. He made his NHL debut in 2000, four years after being drafted. At the time, the six-foot-six goalie was the tallest in league history, but he played only six games for the New York Islanders before being seconded to the minors for another three years before playing once with the Edmonton Oilers. This has been the story of his career—a few games here and there, with plenty of time in the minors as well.

Nonetheless, he seems to have found his niche in recent years as backup to Henrik Lundqvist with the New York Rangers (at least part-time), but throughout his ups and downs and all arounds, he has maintained one insane superstition. The morning of every game he has a bath in a tub full of ice. Think nineteenth-century asylum. Now think twenty-first-century NHL. "It's the last thing anyone wants to do first thing in the morning," Valiquette admitted matter-of-factly one time. "But it's a superstition. I've been doing it since juniors. "

And the point? Well, in his opinion it helps him to visualize the game and keep him sharp as he prepares for the opening faceoff. It's his body, of course, and his superstition, but he's not likely to influence other goalies to follow suit, no matter how many games he plays in the NHL.

PHIL WATSON: Believe It or Not

Phil Watson coached the New York Rangers from 1955 to 1960, some of the worst years in franchise history. He tried what he could as coach to make the team win, but he also believed other elements contributed to the team's poor play. Bob Wolff was a television commentator for the team during Watson's tenure. Before each game he'd come into the Rangers' dressing room and leave his suitcase just inside the door so that when the team had to go to the airport, he'd conveniently have his luggage near at hand.

Watson became convinced this habit of Wolff's was causing defeat for the team and insisted Wolff stop. Wolff agreed, but then when the team went on the ice, he snuck in, put his luggage in the same place, and went back to work calling the game. The Rangers won. Wolff continued doing this for several games and finally told Watson, figuring the coach would see how silly his superstition was. After confessing, he asked Watson if he could simply keep his luggage in the room for the next game as he had always done.

"No!" Watson barked, before adding, "But make sure your suitcase is there."

QUICKSHOT BERNIE WOLFE

Goalie Bernie Wolfe played for the Washington Capitals when they were just about the worst sports team on the planet. One would think he changed superstitions all the time, but one he maintained was certainly as quirky as any. Wolfe wouldn't go onto the ice until the stick boy smacked him on the backside with a stick.

ACKNOWLEDGEMENTS

I'd like to thank the various people who helped put this book together physically and emotionally, starting with the excellent team at M & S. To editor Trena White for proposing the project to me, and to her successor on this title, Liz Kribs. To designer Andrew Roberts for making the words and images mesh effectively and imaginatively on the page. To copy editor Heather Sangster for her keen eye. To my agent, Dean Cooke, and his assistant, Mary Hu, for all of their help with the business side of things. To Darren Boyko, Luke Robitaille, Craig Campbell, Steve Poirier, Phil Pritchard, Izak Westgate, Kehly Sloane, and Kelly Masse (whom every new honoured member at the Hockey Hall of Fame thanks during the telecast because she is so special and helpful and makes every player's weekend such a memorable one). And a special thanks thanks to Dave Dahms, über-Blackhawks fan and world's greatest collector of all things Hawks, for dipping into his photo collection on my behalf. To Carl Lavigne at the Canadiens for much help with dates and info for Habs players. To Szymon Szemberg in Zurich for friendship and nutty Habs talk. And to my family—mom, Liz, Ian, Zachary, Emily, and my wife, Mary Jane, who spends her days saving lives while I push columns around.

PHOTO CREDITS

ANDREW PODNIEKS is the author of more than fifty-five books on hockey. Recent titles include the national best-selling *Canadian Gold: 2010 Olympic Winter Games Ice Hockey Champions; Honoured Canadiens; World of Hockey: Celebrating a Century of the IIHF, 1908-2008; A Canadian Saturday Night; Players: The Ultimate A-Z Guide of Everyone Who Has Ever Played in the NHL;* and *A Day in the Life of the Maple Leafs.* Podnieks also produces media guides for all top IIHF tournaments, notably the Olympics, World Championships, World Women's Championships, and World Junior (U20) Championships. His website is www.andrewpodnieks.com.

Anthem
The Definitive Text

Ayn Rand

Edited by Peter Saint-Andre

Published by the Monadnock Valley Press,
Parker, Colorado
http://www.monadnock.net/

ISBN: 0615876773

ISBN-13: 978-0615876771

Anthem

I

It is a sin to write this. It is a sin to think words no others think and to put them down upon a paper no others are to see. It is base and evil. It is as if we were speaking alone to no ears but our own. And we know well that there is no transgression blacker than to do or think alone. We have broken the laws. The laws say that men may not write unless the Council of Vocations bid them so. May we be forgiven!

But this is not the only sin upon us. We have committed a greater crime, and for this crime there is no name. What punishment awaits us if it be discovered we know not, for no such crime has come in the memory of men and there are no laws to provide for it.

It is dark here. The flame of the candle stands still in the air. Nothing moves in this tunnel save our hand on the paper. We are alone here under the earth. It is a fearful word, alone. The laws say that none among men may be alone, ever and at any time, for this is the great transgression and the root of all evil. But we have broken many laws. And now there is nothing here save our one body, and it is strange to see only two legs stretched on the ground, and on the wall before us the shadow of our one head.

The walls are cracked and water runs upon them in thin threads without sound, black and glistening as blood. We stole the candle from the larder of the Home of the Street Sweepers. We shall be sentenced to ten years in the Palace of Corrective Detention if it be discovered. But this matters not. It matters only that the light is precious and we should not waste it to write when we need it for that work which is our crime. Nothing matters save the work, our secret, our evil, our precious work. Still, we must also write, for — may the Council have mercy upon us! — we wish to speak for once to no ears but our own.

Our name is Equality 7-2521, as it is written on the iron bracelet which all men wear on their left wrists with their names upon it. We are twenty-one years old. We are six feet tall, and this is a burden, for there are not many men who are six feet tall. Ever have the Teachers and the Leaders pointed to us and frowned and said: "There is evil in your bones, Equality 7-2521, for your body has grown beyond the bodies of your brothers." But we cannot change our bones nor our body.

We were born with a curse. It has always driven us to thoughts which are forbidden. It has always given us wishes which men may not wish. We know that we are evil, but there is no will in us and no power to resist it. This is our wonder and our secret fear, that we know and do not resist.

We strive to be like all our brother men, for all men must be alike. Over the portals of the Palace of the World Council, there are words cut in the marble, which we repeat to ourselves whenever we are tempted:

We are one in all and all in one.
There are no men but only the great WE,
One, indivisible and forever.

We repeat this to ourselves, but it helps us not.

These words were cut long ago. There is green mould in the grooves of the letters and yellow streaks on the marble, which come from more years than men could count. And these words are the truth, for they are written on the Palace of the World Council, and the World Council is the body of all truth. Thus has it been ever since the Great Re-birth, and farther back than that no memory can reach.

But we must never speak of the times before the Great Rebirth, else we are sentenced to three years in the Palace of Corrective Detention. It is only the Old Ones who whisper about it in the evenings, in the Home of the Useless. They whisper many strange things, of the towers which rose to the sky, in those Unmentionable Times, and of the wagons which moved without horses, and of the lights which burned without flame. But those times were evil. And those times passed away, when men saw the Great Truth which is this: that all men are one and that there is no will save the will of all men together.

All men are good and wise. It is only we, Equality 7-2521, we alone who were born with a curse. For we are not like our brothers. And as we look back upon our life, we see that it has ever been thus and that it has brought us step by step to our last, supreme transgression, our crime of crimes hidden here under the ground.

We remember the Home of the Infants where we lived till we were five years old, together with all the children of the City who had been born in the same year. The sleeping halls there were white and clean and bare of all things save one hundred beds. We were just like all our brothers then, save for the one transgression: we fought with our brothers. There are few offenses blacker than to fight with our brothers, at any age and for any cause whatsoever. The Council of the Home told us so, and of all the children of that year, we were locked in the cellar most often.

When we were five years old we were sent to the Home of the Students, where there are ten wards, for our ten years of learning. Men must learn till they reach their fifteenth year. Then they go to work. In the Home of the Students we arose when the big bell rang in the tower and we went to our beds when it rang again. Before we removed our garments, we stood in the great sleeping hall, and we raised our right arms, and we said all together with the three Teachers at the head:

> We are nothing. Mankind is all. By the grace of our brothers are we allowed our lives. We exist through, by and for our brothers who are the State. Amen.

Then we slept. The sleeping halls were white and clean and bare of all things save one hundred beds.

We, Equality 7-2521, were not happy in those years in the Home of the Students. It was not that the learning was too hard for us. It was that the learning was too easy. This is a great sin, to be born with a head which is too quick. It is not good to be different from our brothers, but it is evil to be superior to them. The Teachers told us so, and they frowned when they looked upon us.

So we fought against this curse. We tried to forget our lessons, but we always remembered. We tried not to understand what the Teachers taught, but we always understood it before the Teachers had spoken. We looked upon Union 5-3992, who were a pale boy with only half a brain, and we tried to say and do as they did, that we might be like them, like Union 5-3992, but somehow the Teachers knew that we were not. And we were lashed more often than all the other children.

The Teachers were just, for they had been appointed by the Councils, and the Councils are the voice of all justice, for they are the voice of all men. And if sometimes, in the secret darkness of our heart, we regret that which befell us on our fifteenth birthday, we know that it was through our own guilt. We had broken a law, for we had not paid heed to the words of our Teachers. The Teachers had said to us all:

> Dare not choose in your minds the work you would like to do when you leave the Home of the Students. You shall do that which the Council of Vocations shall prescribe for you. For the Council of Vocations knows in its great wisdom where you are needed by your brother men, better than you can know it in your unworthy little minds. And if you are not needed by your brother men, there is no reason for you to burden the earth with your bodies.

We knew this well, in the years of our childhood, but our curse broke our will. We were guilty and we confess it here: we were guilty of the great Transgression of Preference. We preferred some work and some lessons to the others. We did not listen well to the history of all the Councils elected since the Great Re-birth. But we loved the Science of Things. We wished to know. We wished to know about all the things which make the earth around us. We asked so many questions that the Teachers forbade it.

We think that there are mysteries in the sky and under the water and in the plants which grow. But the Council of Scholars has said that there are no mysteries, and the Council of Scholars knows all things. And we learned much from our Teachers. We learned that the earth is flat and that the sun revolves around it, which causes the day and the night. We learned the names of all the winds which blow over the seas and push the sails of our great ships. We learned how to bleed men to cure them of all ailments.

We loved the Science of Things. And in the darkness, in the secret hour, when we awoke in the night and there were no brothers around us, but only their shapes in the beds and their snores, we closed our eyes, and we held our lips shut, and we stopped our breath, that no shudder might let our brothers see or hear or guess, and we thought that we wished to be sent to the Home of the Scholars when our time would come.

All the great modern inventions come from the Home of the Scholars, such as the newest one, which was found only a hundred years ago, of how to make candles from wax and string; also, how to make glass, which is put in our windows to protect us from the rain. To find these things, the Scholars must study the earth and learn from the rivers, from the sands, from the winds and the rocks. And if we went to the Home of the Scholars, we could learn from these also. We could ask questions of these, for they do not forbid questions.

And questions give us no rest. We know not why our curse makes us seek we know not what, ever and ever. But we cannot resist it. It whispers to us that there are great things on this earth of ours, and that we can know them if we try, and that we must know them. We ask, why must we know, but it has no answer to give us. We must know that we may know.

So we wished to be sent to the Home of the Scholars. We wished it so much that our hands trembled under the blankets in the night, and we bit our arm to stop that other pain which we could not endure. It was evil and we dared not face our brothers in the morning. For men may wish nothing for themselves. And we were punished when the Council of Vocations came to give us our life Mandates which tell those who reach their fifteenth year what their work is to be for the rest of their days.

The Council of Vocations came on the first day of spring, and they sat in the great hall. And we who were fifteen and all the Teachers came into the great hall. And the Council

6

of Vocations sat on a high dais, and they had but two words to speak to each of the Students. They called the Students' names, and when the Students stepped before them, one after another, the Council said: "Carpenter" or "Doctor" or "Cook" or "Leader." Then each Student raised their right arm and said: "The will of our brothers be done."

Now if the Council has said "Carpenter" or "Cook," the Students so assigned go to work and they do not study any further. But if the Council has said "Leader," then those Students go into the Home of the Leaders, which is the greatest house in the City, for it has three stories. And there they study for many years, so that they may become candidates and be elected to the City Council and the State Council and the World Council — by a free and general vote of all men. But we wished not to be a Leader, even though it is a great honor. We wished to be a Scholar.

So we awaited our turn in the great hall and then we heard the Council of Vocations call our name: "Equality 7-2521." We walked to the dais, and our legs did not tremble, and we looked up at the Council. There were five members of the Council, three of the male gender and two of the female. Their hair was white and their faces were cracked as the clay of a dry river bed. They were old. They seemed older than the marble of the Temple of the World Council. They sat before us and they did not move. And we saw no breath to stir the folds of their white togas. But we knew that they were alive, for a finger of the hand of the oldest rose, pointed to us, and fell down again. This was the only thing which moved, for the lips of the oldest did not move as they said: "Street Sweeper."

We felt the cords of our neck grow tight as our head rose higher to look upon the faces of the Council, and we were happy. We knew we had been guilty, but now we had a way to atone for it. We would accept our Life Mandate, and we would work for our brothers, gladly and willingly, and we would erase our sin against them, which they did not know, but we knew. So we were happy, and proud of ourselves and of our victory over ourselves. We raised our right arm and we spoke, and our voice was the clearest, the steadiest voice in the hall that day, and we said:

"The will of our brothers be done."

And we looked straight into the eyes of the Council, but their eyes were as cold blue glass buttons.

So we went into the Home of the Street Sweepers. It is a grey house on a narrow street. There is a sundial in its courtyard, by which the Council of the Home can tell the hours of the day and when to ring the bell. When the bell rings, we all arise from our beds. The sky is green and cold in our windows to the east. The shadow on the sundial marks off a half-hour while we dress and eat our breakfast in the dining hall, where there are five long tables with twenty clay plates and twenty clay cups on each table. Then we go to work in the streets of the City, with our brooms and our rakes. In five hours, when the sun is high, we return to the Home and we eat our midday meal, for which one half-hour is allowed. Then we go to work again. In five hours, the shadows are blue on the pavements, and the sky is blue with a deep brightness which is not bright. We come back to have our dinner, which lasts one hour. Then the bell rings and we walk in a straight column to one of the City Halls, for the Social Meeting. Other columns of men arrive from the Homes of the different Trades. The candles are lit, and the Councils of the different Homes stand in a pulpit, and they speak to us of our duties and of our brother men. Then visiting Leaders mount the pulpit and they read to us the speeches which were made in the City Council that day, for the City Council represents all men and all men must know. Then we sing hymns, the Hymn of

Brotherhood, and the Hymn of Equality, and the Hymn of the Collective Spirit. The sky is a soggy purple when we return to the Home. Then the bell rings and we walk in a straight column to the City Theatre for three hours of Social Recreation. There a play is shown upon the stage, with two great choruses from the Home of the Actors, which speak and answer all together, in two great voices. The plays are about toil and how good it is. Then we walk back to the Home in a straight column. The sky is like a black sieve pierced by silver drops that tremble, ready to burst through. The moths beat against the street lanterns. We go to our beds and we sleep, till the bell rings again. The sleeping halls are white and clean and bare of all things save one hundred beds.

Thus have we lived each day of four years, until two springs ago when our crime happened. Thus must all men live until they are forty. At forty, they are worn out. At forty, they are sent to the Home of the Useless, where the Old Ones live. The Old Ones do not work, for the State takes care of them. They sit in the sun in summer and they sit by the fire in winter. They do not speak often, for they are weary. The Old Ones know that they are soon to die. When a miracle happens and some live to be forty-five, they are the Ancient Ones, and the children stare at them when passing by the Home of the Useless. Such is to be our life, as that of all our brothers and of the brothers who came before us.

Such would have been our life, had we not committed our crime which changed all things for us. And it was our curse which drove us to our crime. We had been a good Street Sweeper and like all our brother Street Sweepers, save for our cursed wish to know. We looked too long at the stars at night, and at the trees and the earth. And when we cleaned the yard of the Home of the Scholars, we gathered the glass vials, the pieces of metal, the dried bones which they had discarded. We wished to keep these things and to study them, but we had no place to hide them. So we carried them to the City Cesspool. And then we made the discovery.

It was on a day of the spring before last. We Street Sweepers work in brigades of three, and we were with Union 5-3992, they of the half-brain, and with International 4-8818. Now Union 5-3992 are a sickly lad and sometimes they are stricken with convulsions, when their mouth froths and their eyes turn white. But International 4-8818 are different. They are a tall, strong youth and their eyes are like fireflies, for there is laughter in their eyes. We cannot look upon International 4-8818 and not smile in answer. For this they were not liked in the Home of the Students, as it is not proper to smile without reason. And also they were not liked because they took pieces of coal and they drew pictures upon the walls, and they were pictures which made men laugh. But it is only our brothers in the Home of the Artists who are permitted to draw pictures, so International 4-8818 were sent to the Home of the Street Sweepers, like ourselves.

International 4-8818 and we are friends. This is an evil thing to say, for it is a transgression, the great Transgression of Preference, to love any among men better than the others, since we must love all men and all men are our friends. So International 4-8818 and we have never spoken of it. But we know. We know, when we look into each other's eyes. And when we look thus without words, we both know other things also, strange things for which there are no words, and these things frighten us.

So on that day of the spring before last, Union 5-3992 were stricken with convulsions on the edge of the City, near the City Theatre. We left them to lie in the shade of the Theatre tent and we went with International 4-8818 to finish our work. We came together to the great ravine behind the

Theatre. It is empty save for trees and weeds. Beyond the ravine there is a plain, and beyond the plain there lies the Uncharted Forest, about which men must not think.

We were gathering the papers and the rags which the wind had blown from the Theatre, when we saw an iron bar among the weeds. It was old and rusted by many rains. We pulled with all our strength, but we could not move it. So we called International 4-8818, and together we scraped the earth around the bar. Of a sudden the earth fell in before us, and we saw an old iron grill over a black hole.

International 4-8818 stepped back. But we pulled at the grill and it gave way. And then we saw iron rings as steps leading down a shaft into a darkness without bottom.

"We shall go down," we said to International 4-8818.

"It is forbidden," they answered.

We said: "The Council does not know of this hole, so it cannot be forbidden."

And they answered: "Since the Council does not know of this hole, there can be no law permitting to enter it. And everything which is not permitted by law is forbidden."

But we said: "We shall go, none the less."

They were frightened, but they stood by and watched us go.

We hung on the iron rings with our hands and our feet. We could see nothing below us. And above us the hole open upon the sky grew smaller and smaller, till it came to be the size of a button. But still we went down. Then our foot touched the ground. We rubbed our eyes, for we could not see. Then our eyes became used to the darkness, but we could not believe what we saw.

No men known to us could have built this place, nor the men known to our brothers who lived before us, and yet it was built by men. It was a great tunnel. Its walls were hard and smooth to the touch; it felt like stone, but it was not stone. On the ground there were long thin tracks of iron, but it was not iron; it felt smooth and cold as glass. We knelt, and we crawled forward, our hand groping along the iron line to see where it would lead. But there was an unbroken night ahead. Only the iron tracks glowed through it, straight and white, calling us to follow. But we could not follow, for we were losing the puddle of light behind us. So we turned and we crawled back, our hand on the iron line. And our heart beat in our fingertips, without reason. And then we knew.

We knew suddenly that this place was left from the Unmentionable Times. So it was true, and those Times had been, and all the wonders of those Times. Hundreds upon hundreds of years ago men knew secrets which we have lost. And we thought: "This is a foul place. They are damned who touch the things of the Unmentionable Times." But our hand which followed the track, as we crawled, clung to the iron as if it would not leave it, as if the skin of our hand were thirsty and begging of the metal some secret fluid beating in its coldness.

We returned to the earth. International 4-8818 looked upon us and stepped back.

"Equality 7-2521," they said, "your face is white."

But we could not speak and we stood looking upon them.

They backed away, as if they dared not touch us. Then they smiled, but it was not a gay smile; it was lost and pleading. But still we could not speak. Then they said:

"We shall report our find to the City Council and both of us will be rewarded."

And then we spoke. Our voice was hard and there was no mercy in our voice. We said:

"We shall not report our find to the City Council. We shall not report it to any men."

They raised their hands to their ears, for never had they heard such words as these.

"International 4-8818," we asked, "will you report us to the Council and see us lashed to death before your eyes?"

They stood straight of a sudden and they answered:

"Rather would we die."

"Then," we said, "keep silent. This place is ours. This place belongs to us, Equality 7-2521, and to no other men on earth. And if ever we surrender it, we shall surrender our life with it also."

Then we saw that the eyes of International 4-8818 were full to the lids with tears they dared not drop. They whispered, and their voice trembled, so that their words lost all shape:

"The will of the Council is above all things, for it is the will of our brothers, which is holy. But if you wish it so, we shall obey you. Rather shall we be evil with you than good with all our brothers. May the Council have mercy upon both our hearts!"

Then we walked away together and back to the Home of the Street Sweepers. And we walked in silence.

Thus did it come to pass that each night, when the stars are high and the Street Sweepers sit in the City Theatre, we, Equality 7-2521, steal out and run through the darkness to our place. It is easy to leave the Theatre; when the candles are blown and the Actors come onto the stage, no eyes can see us as we crawl under our seat and under the cloth of the tent. Later, it is easy to steal through the shadows and fall in line next to International 4-8818, as the column leaves the Theatre. It is dark in the streets and there are no men about, for no men may walk through the City when they have no mission to walk there. Each night, we run to the ravine, and we remove the stones which we have piled upon the iron grill to hide it from men. Each night, for three hours, we are under the earth, alone.

We have stolen candles from the Home of the Street Sweepers, we have stolen flints and knives and paper, and we have brought them to this place. We have stolen glass vials and powders and acids from the Home of the Scholars. Now we sit in the tunnel for three hours each night and we study. We melt strange metals, and we mix acids, and we cut open the bodies of the animals which we find in the City Cesspool. We have built an oven of the bricks we gathered in the streets. We burn the wood we find in the ravine. The fire flickers in the oven and blue shadows dance upon the walls, and there is no sound of men to disturb us.

We have stolen manuscripts. This is a great offense. Manuscripts are precious, for our brothers in the Home of the Clerks spend one year to copy one single script in their clear handwriting. Manuscripts are rare and they are kept in the Home of the Scholars. So we sit under the earth and we read the stolen scripts. Two years have passed since we found this place. And in these two years we have learned more than we had learned in the ten years of the Home of the Students.

We have learned things which are not in the scripts. We have solved secrets of which the Scholars have no knowledge. We have come to see how great is the unexplored, and many lifetimes will not bring us to the end of our quest. But we wish no end to our quest. We wish nothing, save to be alone and to learn, and to feel as if with each day our sight were growing sharper than the hawk's and clearer than rock crystal.

Strange are the ways of evil. We are false in the faces of our brothers. We are defying the will of our Councils. We alone, of the thousands who walk this earth, we alone in this hour are doing a work which has no purpose save that we wish to do it. The evil of our crime is not for the human mind to probe. The nature of our punishment, if it be discovered, is not for the human heart to ponder. Never, not in the memory of the Ancient Ones' Ancients, never have men done that which we are doing.

And yet there is no shame in us and no regret. We say to ourselves that we are a wretch and a traitor. But we feel no burden upon our spirit and no fear in our heart. And it seems to us that our spirit is clear as a lake troubled by no eyes save those of the sun. And in our heart — strange are the ways of evil! — in our heart there is the first peace we have known in twenty years.

AYN RAND

II

Liberty 5-3000... Liberty five-three thousand... Liberty 5-3000....

We wish to write this name. We wish to speak it, but we dare not speak it above a whisper. For men are forbidden to take notice of women, and women are forbidden to take notice of men. But we think of one among women, they whose name is Liberty 5-3000, and we think of no others.

The women who have been assigned to work the soil live in the Homes of the Peasants beyond the City. Where the City ends there is a great road winding off to the north, and we Street Sweepers must keep this road clean to the first milepost. There is a hedge along the road, and beyond the hedge lie the fields. The fields are black and ploughed, and they lie like a great fan before us, with their furrows gathered in some hand beyond the sky, spreading forth from that hand, opening wide apart as they come toward us, like black pleats that sparkle with thin, green spangles. Women work in the fields, and their white tunics in the wind are like the wings of sea-gulls beating over the black soil.

And there it was that we saw Liberty 5-3000 walking along the furrows. Their body was straight and thin as a blade of iron. Their eyes were dark and hard and glowing, with no fear in them, no kindness and no guilt. Their hair was golden as the sun; their hair flew in the wind, shining and wild, as if it defied men to restrain it. They threw seeds from their hand as if they deigned to fling a scornful gift, and the earth was a beggar under their feet.

We stood still; for the first time did we know fear, and then pain. And we stood still that we might not spill this pain more precious than pleasure.

Then we heard a voice from the others call their name: "Liberty 5-3000," and they turned and walked back. Thus we learned their name, and we stood watching them go, till their white tunic was lost in the blue mist.

And the following day, as we came to the northern road, we kept our eyes upon Liberty 5-3000 in the field. And each day thereafter we knew the illness of waiting for our hour on the northern road. And there we looked at Liberty 5-3000 each day. We know not whether they looked at us also, but we think they did.

Then one day they came close to the hedge, and suddenly they turned to us. They turned in a whirl and the movement of their body stopped, as if slashed off, as suddenly as it had started. They stood still as a stone, and they looked straight upon us, straight into our eyes. There was no smile on their face, and no welcome. But their face was taut, and their eyes were dark. Then they turned as swiftly, and they walked away from us.

But the following day, when we came to the road, they smiled. They smiled to us and for us. And we smiled in answer. Their head fell back, and their arms fell, as if their arms and their thin white neck were stricken suddenly with a great lassitude. They were not looking upon us, but upon the sky. Then they glanced at us over their shoulder, and we felt as if a hand had touched our body, slipping softly from our lips to our feet.

Every morning thereafter, we greeted each other with our eyes. We dared not speak. It is a transgression to speak to men of other Trades, save in groups at the Social Meetings. But once, standing at the hedge, we raised our hand to our forehead and then moved it slowly, palm down, toward

Liberty 5-3000. Had the others seen it, they could have guessed nothing, for it looked only as if we were shading our eyes from the sun. But Liberty 5-3000 saw it and understood. They raised their hand to their forehead and moved it as we had. Thus, each day, we greet Liberty 5-3000, and they answer, and no men can suspect.

We do not wonder at this new sin of ours. It is our second Transgression of Preference, for we do not think of all our brothers, as we must, but only of one, and their name is Liberty 5-3000. We do not know why we think of them. We do not know why, when we think of them, we feel of a sudden that the earth is good and that it is not a burden to live.

We do not think of them as Liberty 5-3000 any longer. We have given them a name in our thoughts. We call them the Golden One. But it is a sin to give men names which distinguish them from other men. Yet we call them the Golden One, for they are not like the others. The Golden One are not like the others.

And we take no heed of the law which says that men may not think of women, save at the Time of Mating. This is the time each spring when all the men older than twenty and all the women older than eighteen are sent for one night to the City Palace of Mating. And each of the men have one of the women assigned to them by the Council of Eugenics. Children are born each winter, but women never see their children and children never know their parents. Twice have we been sent to the Palace of Mating, but it is an ugly and shameful matter, of which we do not like to think.

We had broken so many laws, and today we have broken one more. Today, we spoke to the Golden One.

The other women were far off in the field, when we stopped at the hedge by the side of the road. The Golden One were kneeling alone at the moat which runs through the field. And the drops of water falling from their hands, as they raised the water to their lips, were like sparks of fire in the sun. Then the Golden One saw us, and they did not move, kneeling there, looking at us, and circles of light played upon their white tunic, from the sun on the water of the moat, and one sparkling drop fell from a finger of their hand held as frozen in the air.

Then the Golden One rose and walked to the hedge, as if they had heard a command in our eyes. The two other Street Sweepers of our brigade were a hundred paces away down the road. And we thought that International 4-8818 would not betray us, and Union 5-3992 would not understand. So we looked straight upon the Golden One, and we saw the shadows of their lashes on their white cheeks and the sparks of sun on their lips. And we said:

"You are beautiful, Liberty 5-3000."

Their face did not move and they did not avert their eyes. Only their eyes grew wider, and there was triumph in their eyes, and it was not triumph over us, but over things we could not guess.

Then they asked:

"What is your name?"

"Equality 7-2521," we answered.

"You are not one of our brothers, Equality 7-2521, for we do not wish you to be."

We cannot say what they meant, for there are no words for their meaning, but we know it without words and we knew it then.

"No," we answered, "nor are you one of our sisters."

"If you see us among scores of women, will you look upon us?"

"We shall look upon you, Liberty 5-3000, if we see you among all the women of the earth."

Then they asked:

"Are Street Sweepers sent to different parts of the City or do they always work in the same places?"

"They always work in the same places," we answered, "and no one will take this road away from us."

"Your eyes," they said, "are not like the eyes of any among men."

And suddenly, without cause for the thought which came to us, we felt cold, cold to our stomach.

"How old are you?" we asked.

They understood our thought, for they lowered their eyes for the first time.

"Seventeen," they whispered.

And we sighed, as if a burden had been taken from us, for we had been thinking without reason of the Palace of Mating. And we thought that we would not let the Golden

One be sent to the Palace. How to prevent it, how to bar the will of the Councils, we knew not, but we knew suddenly that we would. Only we do not know why such thought came to us, for these ugly matters bear no relation to us and the Golden One. What relation can they bear?

Still, without reason, as we stood there by the hedge, we felt our lips drawn tight with hatred, a sudden hatred for all our brother men. And the Golden One saw it and smiled slowly, and there was in their smile the first sadness we had seen in them. We think that in the wisdom of women the Golden One had understood more than we can understand.

Then three of the sisters in the field appeared, coming toward the road, so the Golden One walked away from us. They took the bag of seeds, and they threw the seeds into the furrows of earth as they walked away. But the seeds flew wildly, for the hand of the Golden One was trembling.

Yet as we walked back to the Home of the Street Sweepers, we felt that we wanted to sing, without reason. So we were reprimanded tonight, in the dining hall, for without knowing it we had begun to sing aloud some tune we had never heard. But it is not proper to sing without reason, save at the Social Meetings.

"We are singing because we are happy," we answered the one of the Home Council who reprimanded us.

"Indeed you are happy," they answered. "How else can men be when they live for their brothers?"

And now, sitting here in our tunnel, we wonder about these words. It is forbidden, not to be happy. For, as it has been explained to us, men are free and the earth belongs to them; and all things on earth belong to all men; and the will of all men together is good for all; and so all men must be happy.

Yet as we stand at night in the great hall, removing our garments for sleep, we look upon our brothers and we wonder. The heads of our brothers are bowed. The eyes of our brothers are dull, and never do they look one another in the eyes. The shoulders of our brothers are hunched, and their muscles are drawn, as if their bodies were shrinking and wished to shrink out of sight. And a word steals into our mind, as we look upon our brothers, and that word is fear.

There is fear hanging in the air of the sleeping halls, and in the air of the streets. Fear walks through the City, fear without name, without shape. All men feel it and none dare to speak.

We feel it also, when we are in the Home of the Street Sweepers. But here, in our tunnel, we feel it no longer. The air is pure under the ground. There is no odor of men. And these three hours give us strength for our hours above the ground.

Our body is betraying us, for the Council of the Home looks with suspicion upon us. It is not good to feel too much joy nor to be glad that our body lives. For we matter not and it must not matter to us whether we live or die, which is to be as our brothers will it. But we, Equality 7-2521, are glad to be living. If this is a vice, then we wish no virtue.

Yet our brothers are not like us. All is not well with our brothers. There are Fraternity 2-5503, a quiet boy with wise, kind eyes, who cry suddenly, without reason, in the midst of day or night, and their body shakes with sobs they cannot explain. There are Solidarity 9-6347, who are a bright youth, without fear in the day; but they scream in their sleep, and they scream: "Help us! Help us! Help us!" into the night, in a voice which chills our bones, but the Doctors cannot cure Solidarity 9-6347.

And as we all undress at night, in the dim light of the candles, our brothers are silent, for they dare not speak the thoughts of their minds. For all must agree with all, and they cannot know if their thoughts are the thoughts of all, and so they fear to speak. And they are glad when the candles are blown for the night. But we, Equality 7-2521, look through the window upon the sky, and there is peace in the sky, and cleanliness, and dignity. And beyond the City there lies the plain, and beyond the plain, black upon the black sky, there lies the Uncharted Forest.

We do not wish to look upon the Uncharted Forest. We do not wish to think of it. But ever do our eyes return to that black patch upon the sky. Men never enter the Uncharted Forest, for there is no power to explore it and no path to lead among its ancient trees which stand as guards of fearful secrets. It is whispered that once or twice in a hundred years, one among the men of the City escape alone and run to the Uncharted Forest, without call or reason. These men do not return. They perish from hunger and from the claws of the wild beasts which roam the Forest. But our Councils say that this is only a legend. We have heard that there are many Uncharted Forests over the land, among the Cities. And it is whispered that they have grown over the ruins of many cities of the Unmentionable Times. The trees have swallowed the ruins, and the bones under the ruins, and all the things which perished.

And as we look upon the Uncharted Forest far in the night, we think of the secrets of the Unmentionable Times. And we wonder how it came to pass that these secrets were lost to the world. We have heard the legends of the great fighting, in which many men fought on one side and only a few on the other. These few were the Evil Ones and they were conquered. Then great fires raged over the land. And in these fires the Evil Ones and all the things made by the Evil Ones were burned. And the fire which is called the Dawn of the Great Re-birth, was the Script Fire where all the scripts of the Evil Ones were burned, and with them all the words of the Evil Ones. Great mountains of flame stood in the squares of the Cities for three months. Then came the Great Re-birth.

The words of the Evil Ones ... The words of the Unmentionable Times ... What are the words which we have lost?

May the Council have mercy upon us! We had no wish to write such question, and we knew not what we were doing till we had written it. We shall not ask this question and we shall not think it. We shall not call death upon our head.

And yet ... And yet ...

There is some word, one single word which is not in the language of men, but which had been. And this is the Unspeakable Word, which no men may speak nor hear. But sometimes, and it is rare, sometimes, somewhere, one among men find that word. They find it upon scraps of old manuscripts or cut into the fragments of ancient stones. But when they speak it they are put to death. There is no crime punished by death in this world, save this one crime of speaking the Unspeakable Word.

We have seen one of such men burned alive in the square of the City. And it was a sight which has stayed with us through the years, and it haunts us, and follows us, and it gives us no rest. We were a child then, ten years old. And we stood in the great square with all the children and all the men of the City, sent to behold the burning. They brought the Transgressor out into the square and they led them to the pyre. They had torn out the tongue of the Transgressor, so that they could speak no longer. The Transgressor were young and tall. They had hair of gold and eyes blue as morning. They walked to the pyre, and their step did not falter. And of all the faces on that square, of all the faces which shrieked and screamed and spat curses upon them, theirs was the calmest and the happiest face.

As the chains were wound over their body at the stake, and a flame set to the pyre, the Transgressor looked upon the City. There was a thin thread of blood running from the corner of their mouth, but their lips were smiling. And a monstrous thought came to us then, which has never left us. We had heard of Saints. There are the Saints of Labor, and the Saints of the Councils, and the Saints of the Great Re-birth. But we had never seen a Saint nor what the likeness of a Saint should be. And we thought then, standing in the square, that the likeness of a Saint was the face we saw before us in the flames, the face of the Transgressor of the Unspeakable Word.

As the flames rose, a thing happened which no eyes saw but ours, else we would not be living today. Perhaps it had only seemed to us. But it seemed to us that the eyes of the Transgressor had chosen us from the crowd and were looking straight upon us. There was no pain in their eyes and no knowledge of the agony of their body. There was only joy in them, and pride, a pride holier than it is fit for human pride to be. And it seemed as if these eyes were trying to tell us something through the flames, to send into our eyes some word without sound. And it seemed as if these eyes were begging us to gather that word and not to let it go from us and from the earth. But the flames rose and we could not guess the word....

What — even if we have to burn for it like the Saint of the pyre — what is the Unspeakable Word?

III

We, Equality 7-2521, have discovered a new power of nature. And we have discovered it alone, and we alone are to know it.

It is said. Now let us be lashed for it, if we must. The Council of Scholars has said that we all know the things which exist and therefore the things which are not known by all do not exist. But we think that the Council of Scholars is blind. The secrets of this earth are not for all men to see, but only for those who will seek them. We know, for we have found a secret unknown to all our brothers.

We know not what this power is nor whence it comes. But we know its nature, we have watched it and worked with it. We saw it first two years ago. One night, we were cutting open the body of a dead frog when we saw its leg jerking. It was dead, yet it moved. Some power unknown to men was making it move. We could not understand it. Then, after many tests, we found the answer. The frog had been hanging on a wire of copper; and it had been the metal of our knife which had sent a strange power to the copper through the brine of the frog's body. We put a piece of copper and a piece of zinc into a jar of brine, we touched a wire to them, and there, under our fingers, was a miracle which had never occurred before, a new miracle and a new power.

This discovery haunted us. We followed it in preference to all our studies. We worked with it, we tested it in more ways than we can describe, and each step was as another miracle unveiling before us. We came to know that we had found the greatest power on earth. For it defies all the laws known to men. It makes the needle move and turn on the compass which we stole from the Home of the Scholars; but we had been taught, when still a child, that the loadstone points to the north and that this is a law which nothing can change; yet our new power defies all laws. We found that it causes lightning, and never have men known what causes lightning. In thunderstorms, we raised a tall rod of iron by the side of our hole, and we watched it from below. We have seen the lightning strike it again and again. And now we know that metal draws the power of the sky, and that metal can be made to give it forth.

We have built strange things with this discovery of ours. We used for it the copper wires which we found here under the ground. We have walked the length of our tunnel, with a candle lighting the way. We could go no farther than half a mile, for earth and rock had fallen at both ends. But we gathered all the things we found and we brought them to our work place. We found strange boxes with bars of metal inside, with many cords and strands and coils of metal. We found wires that led to strange little globes of glass on the walls; they contained threads of metal thinner than a spider's web.

These things help us in our work. We do not understand them, but we think that the men of the Unmentionable Times had known our power of the sky, and these things had some relation to it. We do not know, but we shall learn. We cannot stop now, even though it frightens us that we are alone in our knowledge.

No single one can possess greater wisdom than the many Scholars who are elected by all men for their wisdom. Yet we can. We do. We have fought against saying it, but now it is said. We do not care. We forget all men, all laws and all things save our metals and our wires. So much is still to be learned! So long a road lies before us, and what care we if we must travel it alone!

IV

Many days passed before we could speak to the Golden One again. But then came the day when the sky turned white, as if the sun had burst and spread its flame in the air, and the fields lay still without breath, and the dust of the road was white in the glow. So the women of the field were weary, and they tarried over their work, and they were far from the road when we came. But the Golden One stood alone at the hedge, waiting. We stopped and we saw that their eyes, so hard and scornful to the world, were looking at us as if they would obey any word we might speak.

And we said:

"We have given you a name in our thoughts, Liberty 5-3000."

"What is our name?" they asked.

"The Golden One."

"Nor do we call you Equality 7-2521 when we think of you."

"What name have you given us?"

They looked straight into our eyes and they held their head high and they answered:

"The Unconquered."

For a long time we could not speak. Then we said:

"Such thoughts as these are forbidden, Golden One."

"But you think such thoughts as these and you wish us to think them."

We looked into their eyes and we could not lie.

"Yes," we whispered, and they smiled, and then we said: "Our dearest one, do not obey us."

They stepped back, and their eyes were wide and still.

"Speak these words again," they whispered.

"Which words?" we asked. But they did not answer, and we knew it.

"Our dearest one," we whispered.

Never have men said this to women.

The head of the Golden One bowed slowly, and they stood still before us, their arms at their sides, the palms of their hands turned to us, as if their body were delivered in submission to our eyes. And we could not speak.

Then they raised their head, and they spoke simply and gently, as if they wished us to forget some anxiety of their own.

"The day is hot," they said, "and you have worked for many hours and you must be weary."

"No," we answered.

"It is cooler in the fields," they said, "and there is water to drink. Are you thirsty?"

"Yes," we answered, "but we cannot cross the hedge."

"We shall bring the water to you," they said.

Then they knelt by the moat, they gathered water in their two hands, they rose and they held the water out to our lips.

We do not know if we drank that water. We only knew suddenly that their hands were empty, but we were still holding our lips to their hands, and that they knew it, but did not move.

We raised our head and stepped back. For we did not understand what had made us do this, and we were afraid to understand it.

And the Golden One stepped back, and stood looking upon their hands in wonder. Then the Golden One moved away, even though no others were coming, and they moved stepping back, as if they could not turn from us, their arms bent before them, as if they could not lower their hands.

AYN RAND

V

We made it. We created it. We brought it forth from the night of the ages. We alone. Our hands. Our mind. Ours alone and only.

We know not what we are saying. Our head is reeling. We look upon the light which we have made. We shall be forgiven for anything we say tonight....

Tonight, after more days and trials than we can count, we finished building a strange thing, from the remains of the Unmentionable Times, a box of glass, devised to give forth the power of the sky of greater strength than we had ever achieved before. And when we put our wires to this box, when we closed the current — the wire glowed! It came to life, it turned red, and a circle of light lay on the stone before us.

We stood, and we held our head in our hands. We could not conceive of that which we had created. We had touched no flint, made no fire. Yet here was light, light that came from nowhere, light from the heart of metal.

We blew out the candle. Darkness swallowed us. There was nothing left around us, nothing save night and a thin thread of flame in it, as a crack in the wall of a prison. We stretched our hands to the wire, and we saw our fingers in the red glow. We could not see our body nor feel it, and in that moment nothing existed save our two hands over a wire glowing in a black abyss.

Then we thought of the meaning of that which lay before us. We can light our tunnel, and the City, and all the Cities of the world with nothing save metal and wires. We can give our brothers a new light, cleaner and brighter than any they have ever known. The power of the sky can be made to do men's bidding. There are no limits to its secrets and its might, and it can be made to grant us anything if we but choose to ask.

Then we knew what we must do. Our discovery is too great for us to waste our time in sweeping the streets. We must not keep our secret to ourselves, nor buried under the ground. We must bring it into the sight of all men. We need all our time, we need the work rooms of the Home of the Scholars, we want the help of our brother Scholars and their wisdom joined to ours. There is so much work ahead for all of us, for all the Scholars of the world.

In a month, the World Council of Scholars is to meet in our City. It is a great Council, to which the wisest of all lands are elected, and it meets once a year in the different Cities of the earth. We shall go to this Council and we shall lay before them, as our gift, the glass box with the power of the sky. We shall confess everything to them. They will see, understand and forgive. For our gift is greater than our transgression. They will explain it to the Council of Vocations, and we shall be assigned to the Home of the Scholars. This has never been done before, but neither has a gift such as ours ever been offered to men.

We must wait. We must guard our tunnel as we had never guarded it before. For should any men save the Scholars learn of our secret, they would not understand it, nor would they believe us. They would see nothing, save our crime of working alone, and they would destroy us and our light. We care not about our body, but our light is...

Yes, we do care. For the first time do we care about our body. For this wire is as a part of our body, as a vein torn from us, glowing with our blood. Are we proud of this thread of metal, or of our hands which made it, or is there a line to divide these two?

We stretch out our arms. For the first time do we know how strong our arms are. And a strange thought comes to us: we wonder, for the first time in our life, what we look like. Men never see their own faces and never ask their brothers about it, for it is evil to have concern for their own faces or bodies. But tonight, for a reason we cannot fathom, we wish it were possible to us to know the likeness of our own person.

AYN RAND

VI

We have not written for thirty days. For thirty days we have not been here, in our tunnel. We had been caught.

It happened on that night when we wrote last. We forgot, that night, to watch the sand in the glass which tells us when three hours have passed and it is time to return to the City Theatre. When we remembered it, the sand had run out.

We hastened to the Theatre. But the big tent stood grey and silent against the sky. The streets of the City lay before us, dark and empty. If we went back to hide in our tunnel, we would be found and our light found with us. So we walked to the Home of the Street Sweepers.

When the Council of the Home questioned us, we looked upon the faces of the Council, but there was no curiosity in those faces, and no anger, and no mercy. So when the oldest of them asked us: "Where have you been?" we thought of our glass box and of our light, and we forgot all else. And we answered:

"We will not tell you."

The oldest did not question us further. They turned to the two youngest, and said, and their voice was bored:

"Take our brother Equality 7-2521 to the Palace of Corrective Detention. Lash them until they tell."

So we were taken to the Stone Room under the Palace of Corrective Detention. This room has no windows and it is empty save for an iron post. Two men stood by the post, naked but for leather aprons and leather hoods over their faces. Those who had brought us departed, leaving us to the two Judges who stood in a corner of the room. The Judges were small, thin men, grey and bent. They gave the signal to the two strong hooded ones.

They tore our clothes from our body, they threw us down upon our knees and they tied our hands to the iron post.

The first blow of the lash felt as if our spine had been cut in two. The second blow stopped the first, and for a second we felt nothing, then the pain struck us in our throat and fire ran in our lungs without air. But we did not cry out.

The lash whistled like a singing wind. We tried to count the blows, but we lost count. We knew that the blows were falling upon our back. Only we felt nothing upon our back any longer. A flaming grill kept dancing before our eyes, and we thought of nothing save that grill, a grill, a grill of red squares, and then we knew that we were looking at the squares of the iron grill in the door, and there were also the squares of stone on the walls, and the squares which the lash was cutting upon our back, crossing and re-crossing itself in our flesh.

Then we saw a fist before us. It knocked our chin up, and we saw the red froth of our mouth on the withered fingers, and the Judge asked:

"Where have you been?"

But we jerked our head away, hid our face upon our tied hands, and bit our lips.

The lash whistled again. We wondered who was sprinkling burning coal dust upon the floor, for we saw drops of red twinkling on the stones around us.

Then we knew nothing, save two voices snarling steadily, one after the other, even though we knew they were speaking many minutes apart:

"Where have you been where have you been where have you been where have you been..."

And our lips moved, but the sound trickled back into our throat, and the sound was only:

"The light... The light... The light...."

Then we knew nothing.

We opened our eyes, lying on our stomach on the brick floor of a cell. We looked upon two hands lying far before us on the bricks, and we moved them, and we knew that they were our hands. But we could not move our body. Then we smiled, for we thought of the light and that we had not betrayed it.

We lay in our cell for many days. The door opened twice each day, once for the men who brought us bread and water, and once for the Judges. Many Judges came to our cell, first the humblest and then the most honored Judges of the City. They stood before us in their white togas, and they asked:

"Are you ready to speak?"

But we shook our head, lying before them on the floor. And they departed.

We counted each day and each night as it passed. Then, tonight, we knew that we must escape. For tomorrow the World Council of Scholars is to meet in our City.

It was easy to escape from the Palace of Corrective Detention. The locks are old on the doors and there are no guards about. There is no reason to have guards, for men have never defied the Councils so far as to escape from whatever place they were ordered to be. Our body is healthy and strength returns to it speedily. We lunged against the door and it gave way. We stole through the dark passages, and through the dark streets, and down into our tunnel.

We lit the candle and we saw that our place had not been found and nothing had been touched. And our glass box stood before us on the cold oven, as we had left it. What matter they now, the scars upon our back!

Tomorrow, in the full light of day, we shall take our box, and leave our tunnel open, and walk through the streets to the Home of the Scholars. We shall put before them the greatest gift ever offered to men. We shall tell them the truth. We shall hand to them, as our confession, these pages we have written. We shall join our hands to theirs, and we shall work together, with the power of the sky, for the glory of mankind. Our blessing upon you, our brothers! Tomorrow, you will take us back into your fold and we shall be an outcast no longer. Tomorrow we shall be one of you again. Tomorrow...

VII

It is dark here in the forest. The leaves rustle over our head, black against the last gold of the sky. The moss is soft and warm. We shall sleep on this moss for many nights, till the beasts of the forest come to tear our body. We have no bed now, save the moss, and no future, save the beasts.

We are old now, yet we were young this morning, when we carried our glass box through the streets of the City to the Home of the Scholars. No men stopped us, for there were none about from the Palace of Corrective Detention, and the others knew nothing. No men stopped us at the gate. We walked through the empty passages and into the great hall where the World Council of Scholars sat in solemn meeting.

We saw nothing as we entered, save the sky in the great windows, blue and glowing. Then we saw the Scholars who sat around a long table; they were as shapeless clouds huddled at the rise of the great sky. There were men whose famous names we knew, and others from distant lands whose names we had not heard. We saw a great painting on the wall over their heads, of the twenty illustrious men who had invented the candle.

All the heads of the Council turned to us as we entered. These great and wise of the earth did not know what to think of us, and they looked upon us with wonder and curiosity, as if we were a miracle. It is true that our tunic was torn and stained with brown stains which had been blood. We raised our right arm and we said:

"Our greeting to you, our honored brothers of the World Council of Scholars!"

Then Collective 0-0009, the oldest and wisest of the Council, spoke and asked:

"Who are you, our brother? For you do not look like a Scholar."

"Our name is Equality 7-2521," we answered, "and we are a Street Sweeper of this City."

Then it was as if a great wind had stricken the hall, for all the Scholars spoke at once, and they were angry and frightened.

"A Street Sweeper! A Street Sweeper walking in upon the World Council of Scholars! It is not to be believed! It is against all the rules and all the laws!"

But we knew how to stop them.

"Our brothers!" we said. "We matter not, nor our transgression. It is only our brother men who matter. Give no thought to us, for we are nothing, but listen to our words, for we bring you a gift such as has never been brought to men. Listen to us, for we hold the future of mankind in our hands."

Then they listened.

We placed our glass box upon the table before them. We spoke of it, and of our long quest, and of our tunnel, and of our escape from the Palace of Corrective Detention. Not a hand moved in that hall, as we spoke, nor an eye. Then we put the wires to the box, and they all bent forward and sat still, watching. And we stood still, our eyes upon the wire. And slowly, slowly as a flush of blood, a red flame trembled in the wire. Then the wire glowed.

But terror struck the men of the Council. They leapt to their feet, they ran from the table, and they stood pressed against the wall, huddled together, seeking the warmth of one another's bodies to give them courage.

We looked upon them and we laughed and said:

"Fear nothing, our brothers. There is a great power in these wires, but this power is tamed. It is yours. We give it to you."

Still they would not move.

"We give you the power of the sky!" we cried. "We give you the key to the earth! Take it, and let us be one of you, the humblest among you. Let us all work together, and harness this power, and make it ease the toil of men. Let us throw away our candles and our torches. Let us flood our cities with light. Let us bring a new light to men!"

But they looked upon us, and suddenly we were afraid. For their eyes were still, and small, and evil.

"Our brothers!" we cried. "Have you nothing to say to us?"

Then Collective 0-0009 moved forward. They moved to the table and the others followed.

"Yes," spoke Collective 0-0009, "we have much to say to you."

The sound of their voice brought silence to the hall and to the beat of our heart.

"Yes," said Collective 0-0009, "we have much to say to a wretch who have broken all the laws and who boast of their infamy! How dared you think that your mind held greater wisdom than the minds of your brothers? And if the Councils had decreed that you should be a Street Sweeper, how dared you think that you could be of greater use to men than in sweeping the streets?"

"How dared you, gutter cleaner," spoke Fraternity 9-3452, "to hold yourself as one alone and with the thoughts of the one and not of the many?"

"You shall be burned at the stake," said Democracy 4-6998.

"No, they shall be lashed," said Unanimity 7-3304, "till there is nothing left under the lashes."

"No," said Collective 0-0009, "we cannot decide upon this, our brothers. No such crime has ever been committed, and it is not for us to judge. Nor for any small Council. We shall deliver this creature to the World Council itself and let their will be done."

We looked upon them and we pleaded:

"Our brothers! You are right. Let the will of the Council be done upon our body. We do not care. But the light? What will you do with the light?"

Collective 0-0009 looked upon us, and they smiled.

"So you think that you have found a new power," said Collective 0-0009. "Do all your brothers think that?"

"No," we answered.

"What is not thought by all men cannot be true," said Collective 0-0009.

"You have worked on this alone?" asked International 1-5537.

"Yes," we answered.

"What is not done collectively cannot be good," said International 1-5537.

"Many men in the Homes of the Scholars have had strange new ideas in the past," said Solidarity 8-1164, "but when the majority of their brother Scholars voted against them, they abandoned their ideas, as all men must."

"This box is useless," said Alliance 6-7349.

"Should it be what they claim of it," said Harmony 9-2642, "then it would bring ruin to the Department of Candles. The Candle is a great boon to mankind, as approved by all men. Therefore it cannot be destroyed by the whim of one."

"This would wreck the Plans of the World Council," said Unanimity 2-9913, "and without the Plans of the World Council the sun cannot rise. It took fifty years to secure the approval of all the Councils for the Candle, and to decide upon the number needed, and to re-fit the Plans so as to make candles instead of torches. This touched upon thousands and thousands of men working in scores of States. We cannot alter the Plans again so soon."

"And if this should lighten the toil of men," said Similarity 5-0306, "then it is a great evil, for men have no cause to exist save in toiling for other men."

Then Collective 0-0009 rose and pointed at our box.

"This thing," they said, "must be destroyed."

And all the others cried as one:

"It must be destroyed!"

Then we leapt to the table.

We seized our box, we shoved them aside, and we ran to the window. We turned and we looked at them for the last time, and a rage, such as it is not fit for humans to know, choked our voice in our throat.

"You fools!" we cried. "You fools! You thrice-damned fools!"

We swung our fist through the windowpane, and we leapt out in a ringing rain of glass.

We fell, but we never let the box fall from our hands. Then we ran. We ran blindly, and men and houses streaked past us in a torrent without shape. And the road seemed not to be flat before us, but as if it were leaping up to meet us, and we waited for the earth to rise and strike us in the face. But we ran. We knew not where we were going. We knew only that we must run, run to the end of the world, to the end of our days.

Then we knew suddenly that we were lying on a soft earth and that we had stopped. Trees taller than we had ever seen before stood over us in a great silence. Then we knew. We were in the Uncharted Forest. We had not thought of coming here, but our legs had carried our wisdom, and our legs had brought us to the Uncharted Forest against our will.

Our glass box lay beside us. We crawled to it, we fell upon it, our face in our arms, and we lay still.

We lay thus for a long time. Then we rose, we took our box and walked on into the forest.

It mattered not where we went. We knew that men would not follow us, for they never enter the Uncharted Forest. We had nothing to fear from them. The forest disposes of its own victims. This gave us no fear either. Only we wished to be away, away from the City and from the air that touches upon the air of the City. So we walked on, our box in our arms, our heart empty.

We are doomed. Whatever days are left to us, we shall spend them alone. And we have heard of the corruption to be found in solitude. We have torn ourselves from the truth which is our brother men, and there is no road back for us, and no redemption.

We know these things, but we do not care. We care for nothing on earth. We are tired.

Only the glass box in our arms is like a living heart that gives us strength. We have lied to ourselves. We have not built this box for the good of our brothers. We built it for its own sake. It is above all our brothers to us, and its truth above their truth. Why wonder about this? We have not many days to live. We are walking to the fangs awaiting us somewhere among the great, silent trees. There is not a thing behind us to regret.

Then a blow of pain struck us, our first and our only. We thought of the Golden One. We thought of the Golden One whom we shall never see again. Then the pain passed. It is best. We are one of the Damned. It is best if the

Golden One forget our name and the body which bore that name.

VIII

It has been a day of wonder, this, our first day in the forest.

We awoke when a ray of sunlight fell across our face. We wanted to leap to our feet, as we have had to leap every morning of our life, but we remembered suddenly that no bell had rung and that there was no bell to ring anywhere. We lay on our back, we threw our arms out, and we looked up at the sky. The leaves had edges of silver that trembled and rippled like a river of green and fire flowing high above us.

We did not wish to move. We thought suddenly that we could lie thus as long as we wished, and we laughed aloud at the thought. We could also rise, or run, or leap, or fall down again. We were thinking that these were thoughts without sense, but before we knew it our body had risen in one leap. Our arms stretched out of their own will, and our body whirled and whirled, till it raised a wind to rustle through the leaves of the bushes. Then our hands seized a branch and swung us high into a tree, with no aim save the wonder of learning the strength of our body. The branch snapped under us and we fell upon the moss that was soft as a cushion. Then our body, losing all sense, rolled over and over on the moss, dry leaves in our tunic, in our hair, in our face. And we heard suddenly that we were laughing, laughing aloud, laughing as if there were no power left in us save laughter.

Then we took our glass box, and we went on into the forest. We went on, cutting through the branches, and it was as if we were swimming through a sea of leaves, with the bushes as waves rising and falling and rising around us, and flinging their green sprays high to the treetops. The trees parted before us, calling us forward. The forest seemed to welcome us. We went on, without thought, without care, with nothing to feel save the song of our body.

We stopped when we felt hunger. We saw birds in the tree branches, and flying from under our footsteps. We picked a stone and we sent it as an arrow at a bird. It fell before us. We made a fire, we cooked the bird, and we ate it, and no meal had ever tasted better to us. And we thought suddenly that there was a great satisfaction to be found in the food which we need and obtain by our own hand. And we wished to be hungry again and soon, that we might know again this strange new pride in eating.

Then we walked on. And we came to a stream which lay as a streak of glass among the trees. It lay so still that we saw no water but only a cut in the earth, in which the trees grew down, upturned, and the sky lay at the bottom. We knelt by the stream and we bent down to drink. And then we stopped. For, upon the blue of the sky below us, we saw our own face for the first time.

We sat still and we held our breath. For our face and our body were beautiful. Our face was not like the faces of our brothers, for we felt no pity when looking upon it. Our body was not like the bodies of our brothers, for our limbs were straight and thin and hard and strong. And we thought that we could trust this being who looked upon us from the stream, and that we had nothing to fear with this being.

We walked on till the sun had set. When the shadows gathered among the trees, we stopped in a hollow between the roots, where we shall sleep tonight. And suddenly, for the first time this day, we remembered that we are the Damned. We remembered it, and we laughed.

We are writing this on the paper we had hidden in our tunic together with the written pages we had brought for the World Council of Scholars, but never given to them. We have much to speak of to ourselves, and we hope we shall find the words for it in the days to come. Now, we cannot speak, for we cannot understand.

IX

We have not written for many days. We did not wish to speak. For we needed no words to remember that which has happened to us.

It was on our second day in the forest that we heard steps behind us. We hid in the bushes, and we waited. The steps came closer. And then we saw the fold of a white tunic among the trees, and a gleam of gold.

We leapt forward, we ran to them, and we stood looking upon the Golden One.

They saw us, and their hands closed into fists, and the fists pulled their arms down, as if they wished their arms to hold them, while their body swayed. And they could not speak.

We dared not come too close to them. We asked, and our voice trembled:

"How come you to be here, Golden One?"

But they whispered only:

"We have found you...."

"How come you to be in the forest?" we asked.

They raised their head, and there was a great pride in their voice; they answered:

"We have followed you."

Then we could not speak, and they said:

"We heard that you had gone to the Uncharted Forest, for the whole City is speaking of it. So on the night of the day when we heard it, we ran away from the Home of the Peasants. We found the marks of your feet across the plain where no men walk. So we followed them, and we went into the forest, and we followed the path where the branches were broken by your body."

Their white tunic was torn, and the branches had cut the skin of their arms, but they spoke as if they had never taken notice of it, nor of weariness, nor of fear.

"We have followed you," they said, "and we shall follow you wherever you go. If danger threatens you, we shall face it also. If it be death, we shall die with you. You are damned, and we wish to share your damnation."

They looked upon us, and their voice was low, but there was bitterness and triumph in their voice:

"Your eyes are as a flame, but our brothers have neither hope nor fire. Your mouth is cut of granite, but our brothers are soft and humble. Your head is high, but our brothers cringe. You walk, but our brothers crawl. We wish to be damned with you, rather than be blessed with all our brothers. Do as you please with us, but do not send us away from you."

Then they knelt, and bowed their golden head before us.

We had never thought of that which we did. We bent to raise the Golden One to their feet, but when we touched them, it was as if madness had stricken us. We seized their body and we pressed our lips to theirs. The Golden One breathed once, and their breath was a moan, and then their arms closed around us.

We stood together for a long time. And we were frightened that we had lived for twenty-one years and had never known what joy is possible to men.

Then we said:

"Our dearest one. Fear nothing of the forest. There is no danger in solitude. We have no need of our brothers. Let us forget their good and our evil, let us forget all things save that we are together and that there is joy as a bond between us. Give us your hand. Look ahead. It is our own world, Golden One, a strange, unknown world, but our own."

Then we walked on into the forest, their hand in ours.

And that night we knew that to hold the body of women in our arms is neither ugly nor shameful, but the one ecstasy granted to the race of men.

We have walked for many days. The forest has no end, and we seek no end. But each day added to the chain of days between us and the City is like an added blessing.

We have made a bow and many arrows. We can kill more birds than we need for our food; we find water and fruit in the forest. At night, we choose a clearing, and we build a ring of fires around it. We sleep in the midst of that ring, and the beasts dare not attack us. We can see their eyes, green and yellow as coals, watching us from the tree branches beyond. The fires smolder as a crown of jewels around us, and smoke stands still in the air, in columns made blue by the moonlight. We sleep together in the midst of the ring, the arms of the Golden One around us, their head upon our breast.

Some day, we shall stop and build a house, when we shall have gone far enough. But we do not have to hasten. The days before us are without end, like the forest.

We cannot understand this new life which we have found, yet it seems so clear and so simple. When questions come to puzzle us, we walk faster, then turn and forget all things as we watch the Golden One following. The shadows of leaves fall upon their arms, as they spread the branches apart, but their shoulders are in the sun. The skin of their arms is like a blue mist, but their shoulders are white and glowing, as if the light fell not from above, but rose from under their skin. We watch the leaf which has fallen upon their shoulder, and it lies at the curve of their neck, and a drop of dew glistens upon it like a jewel. They approach us, and they stop, laughing, knowing what we think, and they wait obediently, without questions, till it pleases us to turn and go on.

We go on and we bless the earth under our feet. But questions come to us again, as we walk in silence. If that which we have found is the corruption of solitude, then what can men wish for save corruption? If this is the great evil of being alone, then what is good and what is evil?

Everything which comes from the many is good. Everything which comes from one is evil. Thus have we been taught with our first breath. We have broken the law, but we have never doubted it. Yet now, as we walk through the forest, we are learning to doubt.

There is no life for men, save in useful toil for the good of all their brothers. But we lived not, when we toiled for our brothers, we were only weary. There is no joy for men, save the joy shared with all their brothers. But the only things which taught us joy were the power we created in our wires, and the Golden One. And both these joys belong to us alone, they come from us alone, they bear no relation to our brothers, and they do not concern our brothers in any way. Thus do we wonder.

There is some error, one frightful error, in the thinking of men. What is that error? We do not know, but the knowledge struggles within us, struggles to be born.

Today, the Golden One stopped suddenly and said:

"We love you."

But then they frowned and shook their head and looked at us helplessly.

"No," they whispered, "that is not what we wished to say."

They were silent, then they spoke slowly, and their words were halting, like the words of a child learning to speak for the first time:

"We are one... alone... and only... and we love you who are one... alone... and only."

We looked into each other's eyes and we knew that the breath of a miracle had touched us, and fled, and left us groping vainly.

And we felt torn, torn for some word we could not find.

X

We are sitting at a table and we are writing this upon paper made thousands of years ago. The light is dim, and we cannot see the Golden One, only one lock of gold on the pillow of an ancient bed. This is our home.

We came upon it today, at sunrise. For many days we had been crossing a chain of mountains. The forest rose among the cliffs, and whenever we walked out upon a barren stretch of rock we saw great peaks before us in the west, and to the north of us, and to the south, as far as our eyes could see. The peaks were red and brown, with the green streaks of forests as veins upon them, with blue mists as veils over their heads. We had never heard of these mountains, nor seen them marked on any map. The Uncharted Forest has protected them from the Cities and from the men of the Cities.

We climbed paths where the wild goat dared not follow. Stones rolled from under our feet, and we heard them striking the rocks below, farther and farther down, and the mountains rang with each stroke, and long after the strokes had died. But we went on, for we knew that no men would ever follow our track nor reach us here.

Then today, at sunrise, we saw a white flame among the trees, high on a sheer peak before us. We thought that it was a fire and we stopped. But the flame was unmoving, yet blinding as liquid metal. So we climbed toward it through the rocks. And there, before us, on a broad summit, with the mountains rising behind it, stood a house such as we had never seen, and the white fire came from the sun on the glass of its windows.

The house had two stories and a strange roof flat as a floor. There was more window than wall upon its walls, and the windows went on straight around the corners, though how this kept the house standing we could not guess. The walls were hard and smooth, of that stone unlike stone which we had seen in our tunnel.

We both knew it without words: this house was left from the Unmentionable Times. The trees had protected it from time and weather, and from men who have less pity than time and weather. We turned to the Golden One and we asked:

"Are you afraid?"

But they shook their head. So we walked to the door, and we threw it open, and we stepped together into the house of the Unmentionable Times.

We shall need the days and the years ahead, to look, to learn and to understand the things of this house. Today, we could only look and try to believe the sight of our eyes. We pulled the heavy curtains from the windows and we saw that the rooms were small, and we thought that not more than twelve men could have lived here. We thought it was strange that men had been permitted to build a house for only twelve.

Never had we seen rooms so full of light. The sunrays danced upon colors, colors, more colors than we thought possible, we who had seen no houses save the white ones, the brown ones and the grey. There were great pieces of glass on the walls, but it was not glass, for when we looked upon it we saw our own bodies and all the things behind us, as on the face of a lake. There were strange things which we had never seen and the use of which we do not know. And there were globes of glass everywhere, in each room, the globes with the metal cobwebs inside, such as we had seen in our tunnel.

We found the sleeping hall and we stood in awe upon its threshold. For it was a small room and there were only two beds in it. We found no other beds in the house, and then we knew that only two had lived here, and this passes understanding. What kind of world did they have, the men of the Unmentionable Times?

We found garments, and the Golden One gasped at the sight of them. For they were not white tunics, nor white togas; they were of all colors, no two of them alike. Some crumbled to dust as we touched them. But others were of heavier cloth, and they felt soft and new in our fingers.

We found a room with walls made of shelves, which held rows of manuscripts, from the floor to the ceiling. Never had we seen such a number of them, nor of such strange shape. They were not soft and rolled, they had hard shells of cloth and leather; and the letters on their pages were so small and so even that we wondered at the men who had such handwriting. We glanced through the pages, and we saw that they were written in our language, but we found many words which we could not understand. Tomorrow, we shall begin to read these scripts.

When we had seen all the rooms of the house, we looked at the Golden One and we both knew the thought in our minds.

"We shall never leave this house," we said, "nor let it be taken from us. This is our home and the end of our journey. This is your house, Golden One, and ours, and it belongs to no other men whatever as far as the earth may stretch. We shall not share it with others, as we share not our joy with them, nor our love, nor our hunger. So be it to the end of our days."

"Your will be done," they said.

Then we went out to gather wood for the great hearth of our home. We brought water from the stream which runs among the trees under our windows. We killed a mountain goat, and we brought its flesh to be cooked in a strange copper pot we found in a place of wonders, which must have been the cooking room of the house.

We did this work alone, for no words of ours could take the Golden One away from the big glass which is not glass. They stood before it and they looked and looked upon their own body.

When the sun sank beyond the mountains, the Golden One fell asleep on the floor, amidst jewels, and bottles of crystal, and flowers of silk. We lifted the Golden One in our arms and we carried them to a bed, their head falling softly upon our shoulder. Then we lit a candle, and we brought paper from the room of the manuscripts, and we sat by the window, for we knew that we could not sleep tonight.

And now we look upon the earth and sky. This spread of naked rock and peaks and moonlight is like a world ready to be born, a world that waits. It seems to us it asks a sign from us, a spark, a first commandment. We cannot know what word we are to give, nor what great deed this earth expects to witness. We know it waits. It seems to say it has great gifts to lay before us, but it wishes a greater gift from us. We are to speak. We are to give its goal, its highest meaning to all this glowing space of rock and sky.

We look ahead, we beg our heart for guidance in answering this call no voice has spoken, yet we have heard. We look upon our hands. We see the dust of centuries, the dust which hid great secrets and perhaps great evils. And yet it stirs no fear within our heart, but only silent reverence and pity.

May knowledge come to us! What is the secret our heart has understood and yet will not reveal to us, although it seems to beat as if it were endeavoring to tell it?

XI

I am. I think. I will.

My hands... My spirit... My sky... My forest... This earth of mine....

What must I say besides? These are the words. This is the answer.

I stand here on the summit of the mountain. I lift my head and I spread my arms. This, my body and spirit, this is the end of the quest. I wished to know the meaning of things. I am the meaning. I wished to find a warrant for being. I need no warrant for being, and no word of sanction upon my being. I am the warrant and the sanction.

It is my eyes which see, and the sight of my eyes grants beauty to the earth. It is my ears which hear, and the hearing of my ears gives its song to the world. It is my mind which thinks, and the judgment of my mind is the only searchlight that can find the truth. It is my will which chooses, and the choice of my will is the only edict I must respect.

Many words have been granted me, and some are wise, and some are false, but only three are holy: "I will it!"

Whatever road I take, the guiding star is within me; the guiding star and the loadstone which point the way. They point in but one direction. They point to me.

I know not if this earth on which I stand is the core of the universe or if it is but a speck of dust lost in eternity. I know not and I care not. For I know what happiness is possible to me on earth. And my happiness needs no higher aim to vindicate it. My happiness is not the means to any end. It is the end. It is its own goal. It is its own purpose.

Neither am I the means to any end others may wish to accomplish. I am not a tool for their use. I am not a servant of their needs. I am not a bandage for their wounds. I am not a sacrifice on their altars.

I am a man. This miracle of me is mine to own and keep, and mine to guard, and mine to use, and mine to kneel before!

I do not surrender my treasures, nor do I share them. The fortune of my spirit is not to be blown into coins of brass and flung to the winds as alms for the poor of the spirit. I guard my treasures: my thought, my will, my freedom. And the greatest of these is freedom.

I owe nothing to my brothers, nor do I gather debts from them. I ask none to live for me, nor do I live for any others. I covet no man's soul, nor is my soul theirs to covet.

I am neither foe nor friend to my brothers, but such as each of them shall deserve of me. And to earn my love, my brothers must do more than to have been born. I do not grant my love without reason, nor to any chance passer-by who may wish to claim it. I honor men with my love. But honor is a thing to be earned.

I shall choose friends among men, but neither slaves nor masters. And I shall choose only such as please me, and them I shall love and respect, but neither command nor obey. And we shall join our hands when we wish, or walk alone when we so desire. For in the temple of his spirit, each man is alone. Let each man keep his temple untouched and undefiled. Then let him join hands with others if he wishes, but only beyond his holy threshold.

For the word "We" must never be spoken, save by one's choice and as a second thought. This word must never be placed first within man's soul, else it becomes a monster, the root of all the evils on earth, the root of man's torture by men, and of an unspeakable lie.

The word "We" is as lime poured over men, which sets and hardens to stone, and crushes all beneath it, and that which is white and that which is black are lost equally in the grey of it. It is the word by which the depraved steal the virtue of the good, by which the weak steal the might of the strong, by which the fools steal the wisdom of the sages.

What is my joy if all hands, even the unclean, can reach into it? What is my wisdom, if even the fools can dictate to me? What is my freedom, if all creatures, even the botched and the impotent, are my masters? What is my life, if I am but to bow, to agree and to obey?

But I am done with this creed of corruption.

I am done with the monster of "We," the word of serfdom, of plunder, of misery, falsehood and shame.

And now I see the face of god, and I raise this god over the earth, this god whom men have sought since men came into being, this god who will grant them joy and peace and pride.

This god, this one word:

"I."

AYN RAND

XII

It was when I read the first of the books I found in my house that I saw the word "I." And when I understood this word, the book fell from my hands, and I wept, I who had never known tears. I wept in deliverance and in pity for all mankind.

I understood the blessed thing which I had called my curse. I understood why the best in me had been my sins and my transgressions; and why I had never felt guilt in my sins. I understood that centuries of chains and lashes will not kill the spirit of man nor the sense of truth within him.

I read many books for many days. Then I called the Golden One, and I told her what I had read and what I had learned. She looked at me and the first words she spoke were:

"I love you."

Then I said:

"My dearest one, it is not proper for men to be without names. There was a time when each man had a name of his own to distinguish him from all other men. So let us choose our names. I have read of a man who lived many thousands of years ago, and of all the names in these books, his is the one I wish to bear. He took the light of the gods and he brought it to men, and he taught men to be gods. And he suffered for his deed as all bearers of light must suffer. His name was Prometheus."

"It shall be your name," said the Golden One.

"And I have read of a goddess," I said, "who was the mother of the earth and of all the gods. Her name was

Gaea. Let this be your name, my Golden One, for you are to be the mother of a new kind of gods."

"It shall be my name," said the Golden One.

Now I look ahead. My future is clear before me. The Saint of the pyre had seen the future when he chose me as his heir, as the heir of all the saints and all the martyrs who came before him and who died for the same cause, for the same word, no matter what name they gave to their cause and their truth.

I shall live here, in my own house. I shall take my food from the earth by the toil of my own hands. I shall learn many secrets from my books. Through the years ahead, I shall rebuild the achievements of the past, and open the way to carry them further, the achievements which are open to me, but closed forever to my brothers, for their minds are shackled to the weakest and dullest ones among them.

I have learned that my power of the sky was known to men long ago; they called it Electricity. It was the power that moved their greatest inventions. It lit this house with light which came from those globes of glass on the walls. I have found the engine which produced this light. I shall learn how to repair it and how to make it work again. I shall learn how to use the wires which carry this power. Then I shall build a barrier of wires around my home, and across the paths which lead to my home; a barrier light as a cobweb, more impassable than a wall of granite; a barrier my brothers will never be able to cross. For they have nothing to fight me with, save the brute force of their numbers. I have my mind.

Then here, on this mountaintop, with the world below me and nothing above me but the sun, I shall live my own truth. Gaea is pregnant with my child. Our son will be raised as a man. He will be taught to say "I" and to bear the pride of it. He will be taught to walk straight and on his own feet. He will be taught reverence for his own spirit.

When I shall have read all the books and learned my new way, when my home will be ready and my earth tilled, I shall steal one day, for the last time, into the cursed City of my birth. I shall call to me my friend who has no name save International 4-8818, and all those like him, Fraternity 2-5503, who cries without reason, and Solidarity 9-6347 who calls for help in the night, and a few others. I shall call to me all the men and the women whose spirit has not been killed within them and who suffer under the yoke of their brothers. They will follow me and I shall lead them to my fortress. And here, in this uncharted wilderness, I and they, my chosen friends, my fellow-builders, shall write the first chapter in the new history of man.

These are the things before me. And as I stand here at the door of glory, I look behind me for the last time. I look upon the history of men, which I have learned from the books, and I wonder. It was a long story, and the spirit which moved it was the spirit of man's freedom. But what is freedom? Freedom from what? There is nothing to take a man's freedom away from him, save other men. To be free, a man must be free of his brothers. That is freedom. That and nothing else.

At first, man was enslaved by the gods. But he broke their chains. Then he was enslaved by the kings. But he broke their chains. He was enslaved by his birth, by his kin, by his race. But he broke their chains. He declared to all his brothers that a man has rights which neither god nor king nor other men can take away from him, no matter what their number, for his is the right of man, and there is no right on earth above this right. And he stood on the threshold of the freedom for which the blood of the centuries behind him had been spilled.

But then he gave up all he had won, and fell lower than his savage beginning.

What brought it to pass? What disaster took their reason away from men? What whip lashed them to their knees in shame and submission? The worship of the word "We."

When men accepted that worship, the structure of centuries collapsed about them, the structure whose every beam had come from the thought of some one man, each in his day down the ages, from the depth of some one spirit, such spirit as existed but for its own sake. Those men who survived — those eager to obey, eager to live for one another, since they had nothing else to vindicate them — those men could neither carry on, nor preserve what they had received. Thus did all thought, all science, all wisdom perish on earth. Thus did men — men with nothing to offer save their great number — lose the steel towers, the flying ships, the power wires, all the things they had not created and could never keep. Perhaps, later, some men had been born with the mind and the courage to recover these things which were lost; perhaps these men came before the Councils of Scholars. They were answered as I have been answered — and for the same reasons.

But I still wonder how it was possible, in those graceless years of transition, long ago, that men did not see whither they were going, and went on, in blindness and cowardice, to their fate. I wonder, for it is hard for me to conceive how men who knew the word "I," could give it up and not know what they lost. But such has been the story, for I have lived in the City of the damned, and I know what horror men permitted to be brought upon them.

Perhaps, in those days, there were a few among men, a few of clear sight and clean soul, who refused to surrender that word. What agony must have been theirs before that which they saw coming and could not stop! Perhaps they cried out in protest and in warning. But men paid no heed to their warning. And they, these few, fought a hopeless battle, and they perished with their banners smeared by their own blood. And they chose to perish, for they knew. To them, I send my salute across the centuries, and my pity.

Theirs is the banner in my hand. And I wish I had the power to tell them that the despair of their hearts was not to be final, and their night was not without hope. For the battle they lost can never be lost. For that which they died to save can never perish. Through all the darkness, through all the shame of which men are capable, the spirit of man will remain alive on this earth. It may sleep, but it will awaken. It may wear chains, but it will break through. And man will go on. Man, not men.

Here, on this mountain, I and my sons and my chosen friends shall build our new land and our fort. And it will become as the heart of the earth, lost and hidden at first, but beating, beating louder each day. And word of it will reach every corner of the earth. And the roads of the world will become as veins which will carry the best of the world's blood to my threshold. And all my brothers, and the Councils of my brothers, will hear of it, but they will be impotent against me. And the day will come when I shall break all the chains of the earth, and raze the cities of the enslaved, and my home will become the capital of a world where each man will be free to exist for his own sake.

For the coming of that day shall I fight, I and my sons and my chosen friends. For the freedom of Man. For his rights. For his life. For his honor.

And here, over the portals of my fort, I shall cut in the stone the word which is to be my beacon and my banner. The word which will not die, should we all perish in battle. The word which can never die on this earth, for it is the heart of it and the meaning and the glory.

The sacred word:

EGO

ANTHEM

·

Textual Notes

By Peter Saint-Andre

Ayn Rand's novel *Anthem* has had a tangled history. It was originally published in England in 1938, then published again in America in 1946 with a great number of edits. As it was continuously re-published by various printing houses (Caxton Printers in 1953, Signet in 1961, et al.), errors crept in. Those mistakes were further compounded upon its publication on the Internet in 1998. In addition, somewhere along the line the U.S. copyright was allowed to lapse, so it is now in the public domain in America even though it is still under copyright in other countries.

The text presented here is the result of extensive research into the publication history of the novel. Specifically, I completed a word-by-word check of all the published versions, using as my frame of reference the expanded 50th anniversary edition published by Dutton in 1995 (ISBN 0525940154). The Dutton volume helps to clarify Rand's intentions, because it contains both the author's revised American edition (1946) and the original British edition (1938) as marked up by the author during the process of revision. However, I also discovered that the American edition contains edits that are not marked in the Dutton volume, which led me to investigate the provenance of the American edition.

In November 2009, I purchased a second printing of the 1946 edition, issued in February 1947 by Pamphleteers, Inc., of Los Angeles, California. That text answered some questions, but not all. In April 2012, I finally had a chance to inspect the *Papers of Ayn Rand*, MSS81073 in the Manuscript Division of the Library of Congress. This collection contains two texts of interest:

1. A typed manuscript contained in Box 1, Folder 4. This is otherwise unlabelled, but appears to have been an interim version that includes most (but not all) of Rand's edits to the British edition.
2. The galley proofs of the American edition (labelled "REVISE PROOF") contained in Box 1, Folder 5. These are almost certainly Rand's copy (although see the brief note from Ruth E. Meilandt to Rand dated July 23, 1946, which precedes Folder 5 in the papers).

In these notes, the relevant texts are referred to in chronological order by the following letters:

- "B" refers to the British edition of 1938, published by Cassell.
- "T" refers to the 80-page typed manuscript contained in Box 1, Folder 4, of the Papers of Ayn Rand in the Library of Congress.
- "P" refers to the 90-page galley proofs contained in Box 1, Folder 5, of the Papers of Ayn Rand in the Library of Congress.
- "A" refers to the American edition of 1946, published by Pamphleteers, Inc.
- "C" refers to the republication of A made by the Caxton Printers in 1953.
- "S" refers to the Signet (New American Library) paperback edition, first printed in 1961 and reprinted many times since then.
- "D" refers to the 50th Anniversary edition published by Dutton in 1995.
- "G" refers to Project Gutenberg etext #1250, first uploaded to the Internet on 1998-03-01.

Based on my research, I now accept the text of the 1946 edition as canonical. However, in these notes I have drawn attention to any differences between the 1946 edition and the marked-up 1938 edition, the Caxton Printers edition of 1953, the later Signet (New American Library) paperback editions, and Project Gutenberg etext #1250, making reference where necessary to the Dutton volume.

I also reference nameless other editions — now that *Anthem* is in the public domain, it has been reprinted by numerous publishing companies, not all of which have been careful about the text. (It might be surprising that *Anthem* is in the public domain at all, given that it was published first in 1938 and then in 1946; Project Gutenberg has verified that the American copyright was allowed to lapse by Pamphleteers, Inc., but is careful to note that copyright in other countries remains in force.)

This edition includes textual notes only. I have attempted to refrain from any literary or philosophical commentary on the text, no matter how interesting such an endeavor would have been, since that would have unduly expanded the scope of the notes.

Notes to Chapter I

Chapter I, paragraph 3: B and T "only two legs stretched in the mud" vs. P and A "only two legs stretched on the ground". The change from "in the mud" to "on the ground" is not marked by Rand (D 112), although it seems congruent with Rand's outlook (would her hero's feet really be stretched in the mud?) and in any case is more consistent with the later descriptions of the tunnel, which make no mention of mud, muck, mire, or any other combination of dirt and water. Despite the fact that the change is not marked, I follow the 1946 reading.

Chapter I, paragraph 7: Some later editions (including G) have "which we are required to repeat to ourselves" instead of "which we repeat to ourselves", but the three additional words "are required to" are absent from B and A, and are not marked as added by Rand (D 114); therefore I retain the 1938/1946 reading.

Chapter I, paragraph 8: B divides the lines as "only the great / WE, one, indivisible" but there is a note from Rand to the typesetter to move "WE" to the end of the second line (D 114). The change makes sense on metric grounds, because scanning "We are", "There are", "only", the syllables "in-di" of "indivisible", and the syllables "for-ev" of "forever" as two shorts yields three lines of eight feet each.

Chapter I, paragraph 10: Some later editions (including G) have no comma between "the truth" and "for they are written", but the comma is present in B and in A, and is not marked as removed by Rand (D 115); therefore I retain the 1938/1946 reading. B has "Great Re-birth" instead of "Great Rebirth", the hyphen is not marked as removed by Rand (D 115), and the hyphen appears in A. However, C has "Rebirth" with no hyphen (presumably changed from A in accordance with more modern usage), and all editions more recent than C also remove the hyphen. I retain the hyphen for consistency with A.

Chapter I, paragraph 14: B and T have no comma between "five years old" and "we were sent". The comma is not marked by Rand (D 117) but is present in P and in all published editions (A, C, S, G). I follow the 1946 reading.

Chapter I, paragraph 20: Some later editions (including G) have "You shall do what the Council" instead of "You shall do that which the Council", but "that which" is present in B, is not marked as changed to "what" by Rand (D 119), and is present in A; therefore I retain the 1938/1946 reading.

Chapter I, paragraph 22: Some later editions (including G) have "the day and night" instead of "the day and the night", but "the" is present in B, is not marked as removed by Rand (D 122), and is present in A; therefore I retain the 1938/1946 reading.

Chapter I, paragraph 24: Some later editions (including G) have "All of the great modern inventions" instead of "All the great modern inventions", but "of" is absent from B, is not marked as added by Rand (D 122), and is absent from A; therefore I retain the 1938/1946 reading.

Chapter I, paragraph 25: Some later editions (including G) omit the phrase "and that we can know them if we try", but this phrase is present in B, is not marked as removed by Rand (D 123), and is absent from A; therefore I retain the 1938/1946 reading.

Chapter I, paragraph 27: Some later editions (including G) have "The Council of Vocations came in on the first day" instead of "The Council of Vocations came on the first day", but "in" is absent from B, is not marked as added by Rand (D 124), and is present in A; therefore I retain the 1938/1946 reading.

Chapter I, paragraph 28: Some later editions (including G) have "Now if the Council said" instead of "Now if the Council has said", but "has" is present in B, is not marked as removed by Rand (D 124), and is present in A. Some later editions (including G) have "go to work and do not study" instead of "go to work and they do not study", but "they" is present in B, is not marked as removed by Rand (D 124), and is present in A. In both cases, I retain the 1938/1946 reading.

Chapter I, paragraph 32: Some later editions (including G) have "as cold as blue glass buttons" instead of "as cold blue glass buttons", but the second instance of "as" is absent from B, is not marked as added by Rand (D 127), and is present in A; therefore I retain the 1938/1946 reading (where I understand "as" to mean "like").

Chapter I, paragraph 33: B and A "sun-dial" vs. C "sundial", also B and A "one half-hour" vs. C "one-half hour". In both cases the change is not marked by Rand (D 127, 128) and does not occur in A; therefore I retain the 1938/1946 reading.

Chapter I, paragraph 34: Some later editions (but not C, S, or G) have "Thus we lived" instead of "Thus have we lived", but "have" is present in B, is not marked as removed by Rand (D 130), and is present in A. Some later editions have "the children stare" instead of "children stare", but "the" is absent from B, is not marked as added by Rand (D 130), and is absent from A. In both cases I retain the 1938/1946 reading.

Chapter I, paragraph 35: G has "our crime which has changed" instead of "our crime which changed", but "has" is absent from B, is not marked as added by Rand (D 132), and is absent from A. Some later editions (but not G) have "to keep these things to study them" instead of "to keep these things and to study them", but "and" is present in B, is not marked as removed by Rand (D 132), and is present in A. In both cases, I retain the 1938/1946 reading.

Chapter I, paragraph 36: P, A, C, S, and G have "pictures upon the walls" whereas B and T have "pictures upon the walls and upon the floors". When revising the British edition, Rand deleted the second instance of "upon" but she did not delete "the floors" (D 133). Nevertheless, I follow the 1946 reading.

Chapter I, paragraph 37: Some later editions (including G) have "This is an evil thing to say, for it is a great transgression, the great Transgression of Preference" whereas B and A "This is an evil thing to say, for it is a transgression, the great Transgression of Preference"; because the first instance of "great" is absent from B, Rand did not mark its addition (D 133), it is absent from A, and its inclusion can be explained as a simple transcription error, I retain the 1938/1946 reading.

Chapter I, paragraph 44: Some later editions (but not G) have "no law permitting to enter" instead of "no law permitting to enter it", but "it" is present in B, is not marked as removed by Rand (D 135), and is present in A; therefore I retain the 1938/1946 reading.

Chapter I, paragraph 47: Some later editions (including G) have "and we could not believe what we saw" instead of "but we could not believe what we saw". Yet "but" is present in B, is not marked as changed to "and" by Rand (D 136), and is present in A; therefore I retain the 1938/1946 reading.

Chapter I, paragraph 48: Some later editions (including G) have "No man known to us" instead of "No men known to us". But plural "men" is present in B, is not marked as changed to singular "man" by Rand (D 136), and is present in A; therefore I retain the 1938/1946 reading (which is consistent with the lack of singular nouns for humans until Chapter XI).

Chapter I, paragraph 62: Some later editions (including G) have a comma instead of a period between "dared not drop" and "they whispered". But a period is present in B, is not marked as changed to a comma (thus connecting the sentences) by Rand (D 139), and is present in A; therefore I retain the 1938/1946 reading of two sentences separated by a period.

Chapter I, paragraph 65: B and T have "unto the stage" but P, A, and all subsequent editions have "onto the stage". I follow the 1946 reading. Some subsequent editions (including G) have no comma after "Later" whereas B and A have "Later, "; I retain the 1938/1946 reading.

Chapter I, paragraph 66: B and T have "glass vials, and powders, and acids" and "We melt strange metals and we mix acids and we cut open the bodies", whereas P and A have "glass vials and powders and acids" and "We melt strange metals, and we mix acids, and we cut open the bodies". I follow the 1946 reading, despite the fact that the changes are not marked by Rand in her edits to the British edition (D 141).

Chapter I, paragraph 67: B and T "handwritings" vs. P and A "handwriting". I follow the 1946 reading, despite the fact that the change is not marked by Rand (D 142). The change makes sense because the plural would indicate use of the archaic meaning of "handwriting" as "that which is written by hand" (i.e., a manuscript) instead of the modern meaning "a style of writing".

Chapter I, paragraph 68: Some later editions (including G) omit the sentence "But we wish no end to our quest." However, this phrase is present in B, is not marked as removed by Rand (D 143), and is present in A; therefore I retain the 1938/1946 reading.

Chapter I, paragraph 69: P, A, C, S, and G have "no purpose save that we wish to do it" despite the fact that Rand clearly wrote "no purpose save that we want to do it" in her edits to B (D 143) and this is reflected also in T. Nevertheless, I follow the 1946 reading by showing "wish" instead of "want". Some later editions (including G) have "not free for the human heart to ponder", but "not for the human heart to ponder" is present in B and in A, and the addition of "free" was not marked in Rand's edits (D 143); therefore I retain the 1938/1946 reading.

Notes to Chapter II

Chapter II, paragraph 5: Some later editions (including G) have "for the first time we knew fear" instead of "for the first time did we know fear", but "did we know" is present in B, is not marked as removed by Rand (D 147), and is present in A; therefore I retain the 1938/1946 reading.

Chapter II, paragraph 7: P, A, C, S, and G have "looked at" in both instances here, whereas B and T have "looked upon". Rand did not mark "upon" as changed to "at" in her edits to B (D 148). Nevertheless, I follow the 1946 reading. (Note that "look upon" is the much more common construction throughout the text, but is generally used when the looking is more personal or intimate, whereas here Equality 7-2521 is looking at Liberty 5-3000 from afar.)

Chapter II, paragraph 8: Some later editions (including G) have "straight in our eyes" instead of "straight into our eyes", which is present in B, is not marked as changed by Rand (D 148), and is present in A; therefore I retain the 1938/1946 reading.

Chapter II, paragraph 9: C has "were not long looking upon us" instead of "were not looking upon us", but "long" is absent from B, is not marked as added by Rand (D 149), and is absent from A; therefore I retain the 1938/1946 reading.

Chapter II, paragraph 11: C has "their name if Liberty 5-3000" instead of "their name is Liberty 5-3000" as in B, A, S, and G; this is a clear typographical error.

Chapter II, paragraph 12: G has "it is a sin to give men other names which distinguish them from other men", whereas B, A, C, and S have "it is a sin to give men names which distinguish them from other men"; because the first instance of "other" appears to be an error of transcription, I retain the 1938/1946 reading.

Chapter II, paragraph 14: G has no comma after "Today" whereas B, A, C, and S have such a comma ("Today, "); therefore I retain the 1938/1946 reading.

Chapter II, paragraph 15: P, A, C, S, and G have "looking at us", whereas B and T have "looking upon us". As in paragraph 9 above, Rand did not mark "upon" as changed to "at" in her edits to B (D 152). Nevertheless, I follow the 1946 reading.

Chapter II, paragraph 46: G has "shakes with sobs so they cannot explain" instead of "shakes with sobs they cannot explain" as in B, A, C, and S; because the inclusion of "so" appears to be a transcription error in G, I retain the 1938/1946 reading.

Chapter II, paragraph 47: G has "in the dim light of candles" instead of "in the dim light of the candles" as in B, A, C, and S; because the deletion of "the" appears to be a transcription error in G, I retain the 1938/1946 reading.

Chapter II, paragraph 48: G has "our Councils say this is only a legend" instead of "our Councils say that this is only a legend" as in B, A, C, and S; because the deletion of "that" appears to be a transcription error in G, I retain the 1938/1946 reading.

Chapter II, paragraph 49: G has "And in these fires the Evil Ones were burned." However, in B, A, C, and S the text of this sentence is "And in these fires the Evil Ones and all the things made by the Evil Ones were burned." I retain the 1938/1946 reading. Some later editions also omit various other parts of this paragraph (e.g., about the burning of the scripts), but I consider those editions to be clearly in error.

Chapter II, paragraph 51: Some later editions (including G) have "such a question" instead of "such question" as in B, A, C, and S; I retain the 1938/1946 reading.

Chapter II, paragraph 53: G has "but which has been" instead of "but which had been" as in B, A, C, and S; because the change from "had" to "has" appears to be a transcription error in G, I retain the 1938/1946 reading.

Chapter II, paragraph 54: Some later editions (including G) have "led him to the pyre" instead of "led them to the pyre" as in B, A, C, and S; I consider "him" to be a clear error of transcription given that singular pronouns are unknown elsewhere in the novel until Chapter XI.

Notes to Chapter III

Chapter III, paragraph 1: G has "and we are to know it" instead of "and we alone are to know it" as in B, A, C, and S; because Rand did not mark the change (D 167), I retain the 1938/1946 reading.

Chapter III, paragraph 2: G has "all the things which are not known by all" instead of "the things which are not known by all" as in B, A, C, and S; because the inclusion of "all" appears to be a transcription error in G, I retain the 1938/1946 reading.

Chapter III, paragraph 3: P, A, C, S, and G have "a miracle which had never occurred before", whereas B and T have "a miracle which had never occurred upon earth". In her edits to the British edition the only change that Rand marked here was "upon" to "on" (D 169). Nevertheless, I follow the 1946 reading.

Chapter III, paragraph 4: G has "was another miracle" instead of "was as another miracle" as in B, A, C, and S; because Rand did not mark the change (D 169), I retain the 1938/1946 reading (again understanding "as" to mean "like").

Notes to Chapter IV

Chapter IV, paragraph 11: G has "Such thoughts are forbidden" instead of "Such thoughts as these are forbidden" as in B, A, C, and S; because "as these" is not marked as removed by Rand (D 174) and appears to be a transcription error in G, I retain the 1938/1946 reading.

Chapter IV, paragraph 16: G has "those words" instead of "these words" as in B, A, C, and S; because "those" is not marked as changed by Rand (D 175) and appears to be a transcription error in G, I retain the 1938/1946 reading.

Chapter IV, paragraph 28: G has "they knew it but did not move" instead of "they knew it, but did not move", but the comma is present in B, A, C, and S; because the comma is not marked as removed by Rand (D 177) and appears to be a transcription error in G, I retain the 1938/1946 reading.

Notes to Chapter V

Chapter V, paragraph 2: G has "the light which we had made" instead of "the light which we have made" as in A, C, and S; because the addition of "which we have made" is marked by Rand in her edits to the British edition (D 179) and because the change from "have" to "had" appears to be a transcription error in G, I retain the 1946 reading.

Chapter V, paragraph 7: G has "sweeping streets" instead of "sweeping the streets" as in B, A, C, and S; because removal of "the" is not marked by Rand (D 181) and appears to be a transcription error in G, I retain the 1938/1946 reading.

Chapter V, paragraph 10: G has "this wire is a part of our body" instead of "this wire is as a part of our body" as in B, A, C, and S; because "as" is not marked as removed by Rand (D 183) and appears to be a transcription error in G, I retain the 1938/1946 reading (again understanding "as" to mean "like").

Notes to Chapter VI

Chapter VI, paragraph 2: G has "When we remembered" instead of "When we remembered it" as in B, A, C, and S; because the removal of "it" is not marked by Rand (D 185) and appears to be a transcription error in G, I retain the 1938/1946 reading.

Chapter VI, paragraph 3: G has "and our light with us" instead of "and our light found with us" as in B, A, C, and S; because the removal of "found" is not marked by Rand (D 185) and appears to be a transcription error in G, I retain the 1938/1946 reading.

Chapter VI, paragraph 10: G has "then pain struck us" instead of "then the pain struck us" as in B, A, C, and S; because the removal of "the" is not marked by Rand (D 187) and appears to be a transcription error in G, I retain the 1938/1946 reading.

Chapter VI, paragraph 17: C, S, and G have a question mark before the ellipsis ("been?..."), yet the question mark is absent from B, Rand did not mark its addition (D 189), and it is absent from A; therefore I retain the 1938/1946 reading.

Notes to Chapter VII

Chapter VII, paragraph 2: G has "none about the Palace" instead of "none about from the Palace" as in B, A, C, and S; because the removal of "from" is not marked by Rand (D 193) and appears to be a transcription error in G, I retain the 1938/1946 reading.

Chapter VII, paragraph 3: G has "the rise of a great sky" instead of "the rise of the great sky" as in B, T, P, A, C, and S; because the change from "the" to "a" is not marked by Rand (D 194) and appears to be a transcription error in G, I retain the 1938/1946 reading. More significantly, B and M have an extra sentence between "[...] the rise of the great sky." and "There were men whose famous names [...]"; that interpolated sentence reads "There were strange men there, men with white skin like ours, and men with black skin, and men with yellow skin, all dressed alike in white togas." (D 194) This sentence was removed in P and not included in A or subsequent editions. I follow the 1946 reading.

Chapter VII, paragraph 14: G has "placed our glass box on the table" instead of "placed our glass box upon the table" as in B, A, C, and S; because the change from "upon" to "on" is not marked by Rand (D 196) and appears to be a transcription error in G, I retain the 1938/1946 reading.

Chapter VII, paragraph 19: G has "Let us work together" instead of "Let us all work together" as in A, C, and S; because the addition of "all" is marked by Rand (D 197) and its omission in G appears to be a transcription error in G, I retain the 1946 reading.

Chapter VII, paragraph 25: G has "if the Council decreed that you be a Street Sweeper" instead of "if the Councils had decreed that you should be a Street Sweeper" as in B, A, C, and S; because the change from "Councils" to "Council" and the removal of "had" and "should be" are not marked by Rand (D 198) and appear to be transcription errors, I retain the 1938/1946 readings.

Chapter VII, paragraph 26: G has "the thoughts of one and not of many" instead of "the thoughts of the one and not of the many" as in B, A, C, and S; because the removal of "the" is not marked by Rand (D 199) and appears to be a transcription error in G, I retain the 1938/1946 reading.

Chapter VII, paragraph 33: G has "So you think you have found a new power [...] Do you think all your brothers think that?" instead of "So you think that you have found a new power [...] Do all your brothers think that?" as in B, A, C, and S; because the removal of "that" and the addition of "you think" are not marked by Rand (D 200) and appear to be transcription errors, I retain the 1938/1946 readings.

Chapter VII, paragraph 44: P, A, C, S, and G have "pointed at our box", whereas B and T have "pointed their finger at our box". Rand did not mark "their finger" as deleted (D 201). Nevertheless, I follow the 1946 reading.

Chapter VII, paragraph 49: G has "such as is not fit for humans to know" instead of "such as it is not fit for humans to know" as in B, A, C, and S; because the removal of "it" is not marked by Rand (D 202) and appears to be a transcription error in G, I retain the 1938/1946 reading.

Chapter VII, paragraph 52: P, A, C, S, and G have "Then we ran.", whereas B and T have "Then we were up on our feet once more, and we ran." In her edits to the British edition, Rand did not mark "we were up on our feet once more, and" as deleted (D 202). Nevertheless, I follow the 1946 reading.

Chapter VII, paragraph 55: G has "we rose, we took our box, and walked on" instead of "we rose, we took our box and walked on" as in A, C, and S (as edited from the text in B); because the addition of the second comma appears to be a transcription error in G, I retain the 1938/1946 reading.

Chapter VII, paragraph 56: G has "they never entered the Uncharted Forest" instead of "they never enter the Uncharted Forest" as in B, A, C, and S; because the change from "entered" to "enter" is not marked by Rand (D 204) — and because in Chapter II it is mentioned that "once or twice in a hundred years, one among the men of the City escape alone and run to the Uncharted Forest" — I retain the 1938/1946 reading. Furthermore, G has "we wished to be away from the City" instead of "we wished to be away, away from the City" as in B, A, C, and S; because the removal of "away, " is not marked by Rand (D 204) and appears to be a transcription error in G, I retain the 1938/1946 reading.

Chapter VII, paragraph 59: Some later editions omit the sentence "We have not many days to live." However, this sentence is found in B, A, C, S, and G, and is not marked as removed by Rand (D 205), so I retain the 1938/1946 reading.

Notes to Chapter VIII

Chapter VIII, paragraph 2: G has "We wanted to leap to our feet, as we have had to leap to our feet every morning of our life" instead of "We wanted to leap to our feet, as we have had to leap every morning of our life" as in B, A, C, and S; because the addition of the second instance of "to our feet" is not marked by Rand (D 206) and appears to be a transcription error in G, I retain the 1938/1946 reading.

Chapter VIII, paragraph 3: G has "but before we knew it, our body had risen in one leap" instead of "but before we knew it our body had risen in one leap" as in B, A, C, and S; because the removal of the comma is not marked by Rand (D 207) and appears to be a transcription error in G, I retain the 1938/1946 reading.

Chapter VIII, paragraph 4: G has "we went into the forest" instead of "we went on into the forest" as in B, A, C, and S; because the removal of "on" was not marked by Rand (D 208) — and because Equality 7-2521 was already in the forest by this time — I retain the 1938/1946 reading.

Chapter VIII, paragraph 6: G has "the sky at the bottom" instead of "the sky lay at the bottom" as in B, A, C, and S; because the removal of "lay" is not marked by Rand (D 209) as appears to be a transcription error in G, I retain the 1938/1946 reading.

Chapter VIII, paragraph 7: G has "we felt no pity when we looked upon it" instead of "we felt no pity when looking upon it" as in A, C, and S; because Rand changed the text from "it gave us no shame to look upon it" in B to "we felt no pity when looking upon it" in A (D 210) and the change from "looking" in A, C, and S to "we looked" in G appears to be a transcription error in G, I retain the 1946 reading.

Notes to Chapter IX

Chapter IX, paragraph 9: G has "How came you to be in the forest?" instead of "How come you to be in the forest?" as in B, A, C, and S; because the change from "come" to "came" is not marked by Rand (D 213), because "come" is consistent with paragraph 6 ("How come you to be here, Golden One?"), and because the change appears to be a transcription error in G, I retain the 1938/1946 reading.

Chapter IX, paragraph 22: P, A, C, S, and G have "There is no danger in solitude.", whereas B and T have "There is no danger in solitude, and no death." In her edits to B, Rand did not mark ", and no death" as deleted (D 216). Nevertheless, I follow the 1946 reading. Furthermore, G has "there is joy between us" instead of "there is joy as a bond between us" as in B, T, P, A, C, and S; because the removal of "as a bond" was not marked by Rand (D 216) and appears to be a transcription error in G, I retain the 1938/1946 reading.

Chapter IX, paragraph 24: G has "the body of a woman" instead of "the body of women" as in B, A, C, and S; because the change from "women" to "woman" is not marked by Rand (D 217), because use of the plural is consistent with usage of "men" instead of "man" and "women" instead of "woman" until Chapter XI of the text, and because the change appears to be a transcription error in G, I retain the 1938/1946 reading.

Chapter IX, paragraph 26: T, P, A, C, S, and G have "water and fruit", whereas Rand's edits to B have "fruit and water" (D 217). I follow the 1946   reading.

Chapter IX, paragraph 30: G has "as we walk the forest" instead of "as we walk through the forest" as in B, A, C, and S; because the removal of "through" is not marked by Rand (D 220) and appears to be a transcription error in G, I retain the 1938/1946 reading.

Chapter IX, paragraph 31: G has "the good of their brothers" instead of "the good of all their brothers" and "the power created" instead of "the power we created"; because the removal of "all" and "we" are not marked by Rand (D 220) and appear to be transcription errors in G, I retain the 1938/1946 readings.

Chapter IX, paragraph 37: T, P, A, C, S, and G have a comma between "halting" and "like", whereas B has no comma and it is not marked for addition by Rand (D 221). I follow the 1946 reading.

Notes to Chapter X

Chapter X, paragraph 2: G has "we have been crossing" and "rose among cliffs" instead of "we had been crossing" and "rose among the cliffs" as in B, T, P, A, C, and S; because these changes are not marked by Rand (D 222) and appear to be transcription errors in G, I retain the 1938/1946 readings. Furthermore, T, P, A, C, S, and G have no comma between "rock" and "we", yet B has the comma (thus "stretch of rock, we saw great peaks") and it is not marked for removal by Rand (D 222). I follow the 1946 reading. Finally, P, A, C, S, and G have "blue mists as veils", whereas B and T have "blue mists as crowns". Although this change is not marked by Rand (D 223), I follow the 1946 reading.

Chapter X, paragraph 5: G has "the windows went on straight around corners, though how this house kept standing" instead of "the windows went on straight around

the corners, though how this kept the house standing" as in
B, A, C, and S; because the changes are not marked by
Rand (D 224) and appear to be transcription errors in G, I
retain the 1938/1946 readings.

Chapter X, paragraph 6: In her edits to B, Rand clearly
marked a new paragraph at "We turned to the Golden One
and we asked:" (D 225); however, this change was not
reflected in T, P, A or later editions. I follow the 1946
reading. (Subsequent paragraph counts in these notes
ignore the additional paragraph break.)

Chapter X, paragraph 9: G has "we thought it strange"
instead of "we thought it was strange" as in A, C, and S;
because Rand added the words "We thought it was strange
that men had been permitted to build a house for only
twelve." in her edits to B (D 225) and because the removal
of "was" appears to be a transcription error in G, I retain
the 1938/1946 reading.

Chapter X, paragraph 10: G has "colors, colors, and more
colors" instead of "colors, colors, more colors"; because the
removal of "and" was not marked by Rand (D 226) and
appears to be a transcription error in G, I retain the
1938/1946 reading.

Chapter X, paragraph 12: P, A, C, S, and G have "garments,
and the Golden One", whereas B and T have "garments,
rows of garments, and the Golden One". Although "rows
of garments," is not marked for removal by Rand (D 227), I
follow the 1946 reading.

Chapter X, paragraph 13: G has "the letters on their pages
were small and so even" instead of "the letters on their
pages were so small and so even" as in B, A, C, and S;
because removal of the first instance of "so" was not
marked by Rand (D 227) and appears to be a transcription

error in G, I retain the 1938/1946 reading. Furthermore, here again I accept the change from "handwritings" in B and T (D 228) to "handwriting" in P, A, C, and S (see note above on Chapter I, paragraph 67).

Chapter X, paragraph 19: T, P, A, C, S, and G have "asleep on the floor, amidst jewels", whereas B has "asleep on the floor, amidst all the garments they had found, amidst jewels". Although "amidst all the garments they had found," is not marked for removal by Rand (D 230), I follow the 1946 reading.

Chapter X, paragraph 20: Some later versions have "greater gift for us" (or even omit the entire phrase "but it wishes a greater gift from us", as in G); however, B has ", but it wishes a greater gift from us", no changes are marked by Rand (D 231), and the same text is found in A, C, and S. Therefore I retain the 1938/1946 reading.

Chapter X, paragraph 21: Some later versions have "hid the great secrets" but B, A, C, S, and G have "hid great secrets"; because the addition of "the" is not marked by Rand (D 232), I retain the 1938/1946 reading.

Chapter X, paragraph 22: G has "this secret" instead of "the secret" as in B, A, C, and S; because the change from "the" to "this" was not marked by Rand (D 232) and appears to be a transcription error in G, I retain the 1946 reading.

Notes to Chapter XI

Chapter XI, paragraph 15: In her edits to B (D 238), Rand wrote "For the word 'WE' must never be spoken [...]" with "WE" in all capital letters (perhaps echoing the title of Yevgeny Zamyatin's novel *WE*); in A, C, S, and G this is "We" in initial capitals, which I retain for the sake of consistency. G has "and an unspeakable lie" instead of "and of an unspeakable lie" as in the edits to B (D 238) and as in A, C, and S; because the removal of "of" and appears to be a transcription error in G, I retain the 1946 reading.

Chapter XI, paragraph 17: G has "the botched and impotent" and "to bow, to agree, and to obey" instead of "the botched and the impotent" and "to bow, to agree and to obey" as in B, A, C, and S; because the removal of "the" and the addition of the serial comma are not marked by Rand (D 240) and appear to be transcription errors in G, I retain the 1938/1946 readings.

Notes to Chapter XII

Chapter XII, paragraph 6: G has "He took the light of the gods and brought it to men" instead of "He took the light of the gods and he brought it to men" as in B, A, C, and S; because the removal of "he" is not marked by Rand (D 243) and appears to be a transcription error in G, I retain the 1938/1946 reading.

Chapter XII, paragraph 11: G has "dullest among them" instead of "dullest ones among them" as in B, A, C, and S; because the removal of "ones" is not marked by Rand (D 245) and appears to be a transcription error in G, I retain the 1938/1946 reading.

Chapter XII, paragraph 12: G has "the power of the sky" instead of "my power of the sky" as in B, A, C, and S; because the change of "my" to "the" is not marked by Rand (D 245) and appears to be a transcription error in G, I retain the 1938/1946 reading.

Chapter XII, paragraph 13: Some later editions (including G) omit the sentence "Our son will be raised as a man."

However, this sentence is present in B, is not marked as removed by Rand (D 245), and is present in A, C, and S; therefore I retain the 1938/1946 reading. Furthermore, G has "to walk straight on his own feet" instead of "to walk straight and on his own feet" as in B, A, C, and S; because the removal of "and" is not marked by Rand (D 245) and appears to be a transcription error in G, I retain the 1938/1946 reading.

Chapter XII, paragraph 15: Some later editions (but not G) have "This and nothing else." instead of "That and nothing else" as in B (D 247), A, C, S, and G; I retain the 1938/1946 reading.

Chapter XII, paragraph 16: G has "threshold of freedom" instead of "threshold of the freedom" as in B, A, C, and S; because the removal of "the" is not marked by Rand (D 248) and appears to be a transcription error in G, I retain the 1938/1946 reading.

Chapter XII, paragraph 17: B and T have the entirety of this paragraph as "And then came the twilight." (D 248) However, P, A, C, S, and G all have the paragraph as "But then he gave up all he had won, and fell lower than his savage beginning." I follow the 1946 reading.

Chapter XII, paragraph 19: G has "such as spirit existed", "their great numbers" , and "They answered" instead of "such spirit as existed", "their great number", and "They were answered" as in B, T, P, A, C, and S; because these edits are not marked by Rand (D 249) and appear to be transcription errors in G, I retain the 1938/1946 readings. Furthermore, T, P, A, C, S, and G have "all the things they had not created", whereas Rand's edits to B have "all the things which they had not created". Although "which" is not marked for removal by Rand (D 249), I follow the 1946 reading.

Chapter XII, paragraph 20: G has "what they had lost" instead of "what they had lost" as in Rand's edits to B (D 250) and as in A, C, and S; because the inclusion of "had" appears to be a transcription error in G, I retain the 1946 reading.

Chapter XII, paragraph 21: G has "those few" instead of "these few" as in B, A, C, and S; because the change from "these" to "those" is not marked by Rand (D 251) and appears to be a transcription error in G, I retain the 1938/1946 reading.

Chapter XII, paragraph 23: G has "break the chains" instead of "break all the chains" as in Rand's edits to B (D 252) and as in A, C, and S; because the removal of "all" appears to be a transcription error in G, I retain the 1938/1946 reading.

Chapter XII, paragraph 24: G has "I shall fight" instead of "shall I fight" as in B, A, C, and S; because the change from "shall I" to "I shall" is not marked by Rand (D 252) and appears to be a transcription error in G, I retain the 1938/1946 reading. At the end of this paragraph, B and T have "For the freedom of Man. For his right. For his honour. For his glory." In her edits to B, Rand removed the final sentence, changed "honour" to "honor", changed "right" to "rights", and interpolated a new sentence between the first and the second, reading "For his life." (D 252). In P and A, the interpolated sentence is not second (as indicated by Rand) but third, resulting in the text "For the freedom of Man. For his rights. For his life. For his honor." All subsequent editions (C, S, G, etc.) follow A here. I follow the 1946 reading.

8917039R00061

Made in the USA
San Bernardino, CA
26 February 2014